Wagner and the Wonder of Art
An Introduction to *Die Meistersinger*

Richard Wagner's *Die Meistersinger* has always called forth superlatives from those who have fallen under its spell. Toscanini wanted to lay his baton down for the last time only after he had conducted a performance of it. Paderewski called it 'the greatest work of genius ever achieved by any artist in any field of human endeavour.' H.L. Mencken declared, 'It took more skill to plan and write it than it took to plan and write the whole canon of Shakespeare.'

And yet Wagner's many-splendoured comedy has come under severe criticism in recent years for what has been called its 'dark underside,' its 'fascist brutality,' and its 'ugly anti-Semitism.' In *Wagner and the Wonder of Art*, renowned opera expert M. Owen Lee addresses that criticism. He also provides an introduction to the opera and an analysis that will surprise even those veteran operagoers who may not have explored the work's intricate structure and the emotional drama at its centre. The book includes the on-air commentary that Father Lee gave during the first radio broadcast from the Metropolitan Opera after the events of 9/11. He thought it necessary, after attempting to refute the charges leveled against Wagner's opera, to say something about its truthfulness, its life-affirming music, its insight into the madness that can destroy human lives, and its witness to the importance of art for the survival of our civilizations.

M. OWEN LEE is a Catholic priest, professor emeritus of Classics at St Michael's College, University of Toronto, and the author of many books on literature and music.

WAGNER AND THE WONDER OF ART

An Introduction to
Die Meistersinger

M. OWEN LEE

UNIVERSITY OF TORONTO PRESS
Toronto Buffalo London

© University of Toronto Press Incorporated 2007
Toronto Buffalo London
Printed in Canada

ISBN 978-0-8020-9857-3 (cloth)
ISBN 978-0-8020-9573-2 (paper)

Printed on acid-free paper

Library and Archives Canada Cataloguing in Publication

Lee, M. Owen, 1930–
Wagner and the wonder of art : an introduction to Die Meistersinger /
M. Owen Lee.

Includes bibliographical references, discography and index.
ISBN 978-0-8020-9857-3 (bound)
ISBN 978-0-8020-9573-2 (pbk.)

1. Wagner, Richard, 1913–1883. Meistersinger von Nürnberg.   I. Title.

ML410.W16L479 2007   782.1   C2007-905353-X

University of Toronto Press acknowledges the financial assistance to
its publishing program of the Canada Council for the Arts and the
Ontario Arts Council.

University of Toronto Press acknowledges the financial support for
its publishing activities of the Government of Canada through the
Book Publishing Industry Development Program (BPIDP).

for

JOHN, ROBERT, VINCENT, and MATTHEW

and their families

CONTENTS

PREFACE

I have published this book for two reasons. First, many people have asked me to make generally available a lecture I have given on Wagner's *Die Meistersinger* on numerous occasions over the past forty years in Canada and the United States. The lecture was based in part on a piece I wrote for *Opera News* in 1968 that subsequently appeared in the Bayreuth *Meistersinger* program. When I wrote the piece there were few complete recordings of the opera, and the translations provided in them were a half-century old, made for singing, and couched in antiquated and sometimes unintelligible English. Staged performances outside of the major operatic centres were rare, and of course they provided no surtitles. Most opera lovers were entranced by the music of *Die Meistersinger* but had little idea of the richness of its text and of how that text interacted with the music. And because virtually all performances outside of German-speaking lands were heavily cut (there were as many as twenty cuts, large and small, in some performances I saw in North America), most audiences had little idea of the intricate structure of the work, or of the emotional drama at its centre.

Today, with many complete recordings, DVDs, and stage performances available, all of them supplying translations of the text via sub- or sur- or supertitles, that situation no longer obtains, and much of what I first wrote on

Wagner's opera is now common knowledge. Nonetheless, I have not changed much of my original talk here except to rework it for a reading, rather than for a listening, public, and to add endnotes that will point the reader toward further dimensions in a work of art that seems, even after years of listening, inexhaustible.

The other reason for this book's appearance is to provide an answer to the charge, which has gathered force in recent years, that there is a 'dark underside,' a fascist brutality, an ugly anti-Semitic level, in *Die Meistersinger*. Not without revulsion for the distasteful task that is now required of anyone attempting to write about Wagner's masterwork, I have lifted a few pertinent paragraphs from my original talk, expanded and updated them, and transferred them to a separate chapter called, appropriately enough, 'Controversies' – in the hope that this volume will play a part in ending those controversies for good.

Finally, I have added, as a chapter in its own right, the on-air commentary on the wisdom of *Die Meistersinger* that I gave to millions of listeners around the world during the first Metropolitan Opera broadcast after the destruction of the World Trade Center in New York. Even at the cost of repeating what I had already said earlier in the book, it seemed necessary, after attempting to refute the false charges levelled against Wagner's opera, to say something about its truthfulness, its life-affirming music, its insight into the madness that can destroy human lives, and its witness to the importance of art for the survival of our civilizations.

Some of the material in this book has appeared, in

slightly different form, in two of my other volumes, *First Intermissions* and *Wagner: The Terrible Man and His Truthful Art*. I must thank Amadeus Press and the University of Toronto Press for permission to adapt that material for use here. I would also like to thank Suzanne Rancourt, John St James, and Barb Porter of the University of Toronto Press, Iain Scott for providing recordings and DVDs, Father Doug Hilmer for expert computer guidance, and Fathers Allan Smith and Dan Donovan for help in taming, in my translations, Walther von Stolzing's Romantically effusive German verses. I must take full responsibility for the translations of 'Füsschen,' 'schlimmes Weib,' and 'übler Schwäch' in Hans Sachs's cobbling song; the cobbler seems to me to be only twitting the lovers there, not chastising them. But I may be wrong; Wagner's shoemaker seems always to be a step or two ahead of the rest of us.

WAGNER AND THE WONDER OF ART:
AN INTRODUCTION TO
DIE MEISTERSINGER

CHAPTER ONE

The First Stollen

Wagner's *Die Meistersinger von Nürnberg, The Master-singers of Nuremberg,* is a hymn to music – Germany's music first, but finally the music of any land, so long as it is music fashioned out of both art and nature, inspiration and hard work, innovating spirit and respect for tradition. It is also a hymn to all of us, from whatever land, who have felt the joy of being human. And finally it is a hymn to that historical figure who, if I may speak of having a role model at age seventy-seven, has long been a role model for me, a master teacher and a good man who helps others and loves music with all his soul – Nuremberg's beloved Hans Sachs.

I always think of *Die Meistersinger,* all five hours of it, as of some great illuminated medieval song book, with sacred and secular melodies following each other page on page, for hundreds and hundreds of pages. As in those storybook movies I saw in my childhood, some unseen hand pulls the immense score open at the first note of the overture, and then the pages turn of themselves, and the melodies pour forth in wondrous profusion, and the irresistible onward movement through the pages keeps me breathless before the great work, through all its designs and devices, its crotchets and hemidemisemiquavers, its illuminations, its recapitulations, its shining images, the soliloquies and discourses of its endearingly human characters, the pain and laughter and wisdom of it – till the last page echoes the first.

It is difficult to speak of *Die Meistersinger* without using a superlative of some sort. It is, for one thing, the longest of all the operas in the standard repertory – at least according to *The Guinness Book of World Records,* where

Reginald Goodall's performance clocks in at five hours and fifteen minutes, not counting intermissions. And for several years the *Meistersinger* overture was the most often performed piece of music in North American concert halls – at least according to annual trade figures from Broadcast Music Incorporated. *Die Meistersinger* can also lay strong claim to having 'the greatest libretto ever written' – at least that is what Patrick J. Smith says in his authoritative history of librettos, *The Tenth Muse*.

But many Wagnerites at the Wagner festival in Bayreuth will use a superlative from the other end of the scale. They like it least of all the Master's works. I have heard it called 'too German' there, and 'too diatonic,' and even 'too shallow.' Whatever the objection, it is thought by some disciples to be a lesser work of the Master. Not surprisingly, with those whom we may call non-Wagnerites, *Die Meistersinger* is often cited as Wagner's one relatively healthy product, a sort of anomalous accident, and – to use a superlative again – quite the most acceptable of his works.

Finally, there are those of us who, when pressed, would use a more personal sort of superlative: favourite. We would give *Die Meistersinger* pride of place in any roll call of works for the musical stage. And we're not all of us Germans. Among our number is the Englishman who was once head of music for the BBC, John Culshaw, and the Italian maestro Arturo Toscanini, who wanted to lay down his baton finally only after conducting *Die Meistersinger*, and the Polish pianist and patriot Ignacy Jan Paderewski, who cited *Die Meistersinger* as 'the greatest work of genius ever achieved by any artist in any field of

human endeavor,' and the American provocateur H.L.
Mencken, who thought *Die Meistersinger* 'the greatest single work of art ever produced by man,' and added, 'It
took more skill to plan and write it that it took to plan and
write the whole canon of Shakespeare.' At this point Hans
Sachs, the central figure in the opera, would surely say, as
he says about himself near the opera's end, 'Gebt ihr mir
Armen zu viel Ehr' – 'You're giving this poor fellow too
much praise.' Sachs knows as well as anyone that while
past traditions have their claims to greatness, future generations will build on whatever his own era can achieve.

The idea of writing an opera about the sixteenth-century shoemaker-poet Hans Sachs and the mastersingers
of old Nuremberg first came to Wagner when he was a
young man, in the summer of 1845. He had just written
Tannhäuser, but he hadn't yet got it on the stage. He was a
nervous wreck that summer, and his doctor prescribed a
cure at Marienbad, the famous spa in Bohemia, with
orders to do no writing or composing. The weather was
glorious, and he had a good book to read – by Wolfram
von Eschenbach, the poet he had made a character in
Tannhäuser. Wolfram would make nice, relaxing reading
in the woods and by the streams.

But, as anyone who knows Wagner could confidently
predict, he was carried away when he started to read
Wolfram's epic, *Parzifal*, and the related legend of Parzifal's son, Lohengrin. Two potential operas started welling
up in him so urgently that, to distract himself, he turned
to another book, Gervinus's *History of German Literature*.[1]
And before long he was drafting, out of that, a third
potential opera. Just a little thing, really, about the mas-

tersingers of Nuremberg. Only a comedy, so his doctor couldn't really object to his outlining the plot, could he? Besides, it would put all of Wolfram's romantic knights, those Parzifals and Lohengrins, out of his head for a while.[2] It could be performed, this little comedy, as a diversion after festive performances of the three acts of his mighty *Tannhäuser.* It would be like the little satyr play that always followed the three great tragedies in classic Athens. And it would fit nicely with his *Tannhäuser. Tannhäuser* was about a singing contest among the minnesingers of the Wartburg; this would be about a singing contest among the mastersingers of Nuremberg.[3]

So the thirty-three-year-old Wagner started work on the projects that were going to occupy him for most of the rest of his life. He was settling into his bath at Marienbad one afternoon when Wolfram's knights came back with a vengeance and, as he records, he jumped out of the bath and, hardly stopping to pull on his clothes, ran to get paper and pen. The text of *Lohengrin* had to be got down before it went out of his head. Then, as his doctor gave up on him, the music of the love duet from *Lohengrin* started to form in the margin of the text.

After that, through *Lohengrin* and revolution in Dresden and flight from Germany and political exile in Switzerland and endless prose writings and heaven knows how many stormy love affairs, Wagner wrote *Das Rheingold* and *Die Walküre* and most of *Siegfried* and all of *Tristan und Isolde.* And finally, more than twenty years after the idea first came to him, he composed *Die Meistersinger.* All along he had carried the idea of an opera about the mastersingers around with him, and it grew within him. A famous scene in the opera came out of a personal experience: one night, in a tavern in Nuremberg, he was witness to, and to an extent was responsible for, a demonstration of bad singing that exploded into a brawl, spilled over into the street, and was dispersed only when one of the rioters was knocked senseless to the ground, leaving Wagner and his brother-in-law to walk the moonlit streets of the old town in peace. The memory of that night became the pandemonious free-for-all and subsequent midsummer stillness at the end of Act II of the opera-to-be.[4]

Wagner wrote the text of *Die Meistersinger*, his longest libretto, in a month's time, in Paris, where, as always, his disappointments filled him with an intense longing for all things German – for the tales of E.T.A. Hoffmann,[5] the art of Dürer, the winding cobbled streets of old Nuremberg, and the writings of the poet Hans Sachs who lived there when the city was a thriving centre famous for its craftsmanship, its toy shops, its learning, and its works of art. (For two centuries previous Nuremberg had been, as much as any city in Europe, the capital of the Holy Roman Empire, and it had turned Protestant during the Reformation with all of its art treasures intact.)[6] Wagner was able to draw from centuries-old books – the 1571 *Account of the German Mastersong*, by Hans Sachs's pupil Adam Puschmann, and Johann Christoph Wagenseil's 1697 *Nuremberg Chronicle* – as well as from the more recent (1811) *On the Old German Mastersongs*, by Jacob Grimm, for extensive details about Nuremberg's sixteenth-century mastersingers, their rules and procedures, even their actual names. Wagenseil also provided Wagner some examples of the tunes they wrote, a few of which he adapted for his purposes.[7]

Wagner modelled much of the verse for his new libretto after the irregular rhymed couplets, the 'Knittelvers,' that the historical Hans Sachs once wrote – the folksy doggerel that never lost literary respectability in Germany. (Goethe used it for an early poem about Hans Sachs[8] and sprinkled examples of it throughout his *Faust*.) The plot of *Meistersinger* owes something, as we shall see, to the old Roman comedies of Plautus and Terence, and may owe even more to an operetta by Lortzing called *Hans Sachs*,[9] but Wagner, using patterned imagery, philosophical depth, and a flood of great music, turned the plot into a many-levelled work of art that, more than a century later, continues to yield new meanings.

As always with Wagner, the music came after the text, but it came quickly, even though Wagner, disgraced in Munich and living in semi-exile in Switzerland, was going through perhaps the most chaotic period of his life. 'It is my finest work,' he said as he composed. 'I weep and I laugh over it.' He worked at it with the song-filled quickness of a Mozart, a Schubert. He found a dedicated young man, Hans Richter, twenty-four, a horn player in the Vienna Opera orchestra, who was willing to come and live with him and his wife Cosima on Lake Lucerne. (Richter was later to become one of the greatest of all conductors.) In a room upstairs over the composer's, Richter copied sheet after sheet of the massive score as it was passed up to him. And, as the work sped on, he wondered: Wagner was scoring for virtually the same orchestra as Beethoven had in the fifth symphony, with only three additional brass players and a harp added. Yet how new was the orchestral effect! The opera was to have its own special sound – a rich, mellow ripeness altogether removed from *Lohengrin*'s silvery-blue beauty, and the *Ring*'s natural world of sounding rivers and trees, and *Tristan*'s feverish, surging chromaticism. Here the overall impression was diatonic, in solid C-major, with old German archaisms blending effortlessly into Wagner's new, resounding Romanticism. Franz Lizst played the entire piano score through in a single evening, exclaiming over and over on its beauty. Hans von Bülow, preparing the orchestra in Munich, wrote to a friend, 'You cannot begin to imagine its wealth of music, the Cellini-workmanship in every detail. Wagner is the greatest composer, easily the equal of Beethoven and Bach, and more besides.' There *is* much in the score that suggests Beethoven and Bach; von Bülow had struck a kind of composer's trinity – though later, after he had granted his wife Cosima a divorce so she could marry Wagner, he made a new trinity. He coined the phrase, still current, 'Bach, Beethoven, and *Brahms*.'

The overture to *Die Meistersinger* was composed – and performed – before the rest of the music was written. This is altogether remarkable, as the overture (or prelude, as Wagner called it) is a musical summing up of the five-hour work that was to follow. It is the sort of thing an average composer would write last, after everything else was done – assuming that an average composer could write something like *Die Meistersinger*. The first theme, proud and affirmative, in that fundamental key of Western music, C-major, is associated in the opera with the mastersingers themselves, their traditions and their glorious role of preserving their country's artistic heritage:

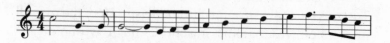

(A few minutes later in the overture, because Wagner's Nuremberg masters sometimes descend to petty concerns and lose sight of larger issues, that theme will be parodied.)

Next we hear the lyric strain that will accompany the amorous glances exchanged by the hero and heroine – furtively, in church.

Then comes a theme derived from an actual mastersinger tune, the so-called Long Tune, associated in the opera with of the mastersingers' waving banner:

Then a confident strain emerges, associated with art:

And finally we hear, in E-major, a key set apart from the C-major tonality of the masters, the new 'Prize Song' that, at the end of the opera, the masters will come to acknowledge as a thing of beauty:

The development of these five themes and three subsidiary ones is a musical marvel, the climax of which is reached when the Prize Song is drawn into the masters' C-major, and played simultaneously with their theme and the theme of their banner. It is a demonstration of counterpoint unequalled in the nineteenth century, and it comes from a man whose enemies had always said knew no counterpoint. The climactic passage also makes an aesthetic point essential to the opera: the Prize Song rides confidently above the tunes of the old masters, altogether new yet melodically and harmonically in conformity with the themes that represent their venerable rules and traditions. New art can build on old traditions and transcend them. Soon the three themes are swept along triumphantly by the confident theme associated with art.

The overture is thus a summation of the five-hour opera to follow, with one remarkable exception: it makes no mention of the opera's leading character, the shoemaker-poet Hans Sachs. Perhaps that is why, when the curtain rises, the music proceeds without a break directly into a chorale sung in church by the people of Nuremberg on the eve of the feast of John the Baptist – who in the allegorical scheme of the opera will be a figure representing Hans Sachs. The chorale, asking for the Baptist's help, is actually a variant on the first theme of the overture. This:

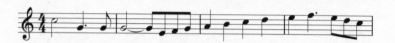

becomes this:

Why did Wagner choose to put the action of the opera entirely on the eve and the feast of John the Baptist? One reason, certainly, is that the feast of John the Baptist, 'Johannistag,' is also 'Midsummer Day,' and on the eve of that day evil spirits were thought to fare abroad, only to be dispersed on the morning by good St John. We are going to witness a couple of brawls prompted in the evening by evil spirits, and our hero is going to get his inspiration in a midsummer night's dream, and in the morning, with the benevolent intercession of John the Baptist, the evil spirits will give way to benevolent ones.

But there is a subtler reason for setting the opera on Johannistag. St John's day is a day important for the fundamentals of music. The notes of the scale – originally ut-re-mi-fa-sol-la-mi-ut – were first named, by the Benedictine monk Guido d'Arezzo, from the opening syllables in each line of the old Latin hymn for the Vespers of John the Baptist's eve:

> *ut* queant laxis
> *re*sonare fibris
> *mi*ra gestorum
> *fa*muli tuorum
> *sol*ve polluti
> *la*bii reatum
> San*cte* Johannes.

(When *ut* eventually proved a little flat, *do* was substituted, from the word that begins so many Latin prayers, *Domine*.)

Wagner's Nuremberg is a city whose citizens have kept such things alive.[10] They have respected tradition and art and music while emperors and princes elsewhere in Germany have let them languish. They are also a devout community, and, as the curtain rises, the church is crowded with people singing Vespers.[11] In fact, they are singing a German version of the Latin hymn that gave us ut-re-mi-fa-sol-la-ti-ut, the hymn to John the Baptist:

> Once our Savior came to thee,
> By thy hand baptized to be.
> Gave himself for our release,
> Teaching us his law of peace.
> Baptist, let us share thy rite,
> And be sinless in his sight.
>> Baptist, teacher, Christ's first preacher,
>> Take us by the hand, there on Jordan's strand.

Between the lines of this hymn, a young man better dressed than the other worshippers has been exchanging glances, from behind a pillar, with a shy and lovely girl who is seated with her nurse in the front pew. When the hymn ends, the organ sounds a pedal point, and the congregation files out. The young man approaches the girl. Her nurse tries to intervene, but he is persistent, and forward enough eventually to ask the question, 'Are you promised to anyone?' The nurse, taken aback, admits, 'It's still a secret, and it's all a little complicated, but yes – she is.' And the young girl hurries to add, 'But nobody yet has seen the bridegroom.'

The girl, we discover, is named Eva. She is the daughter of the richest man in Nuremberg, Veit Pogner, the local goldsmith. Like Shakespeare's Juliet, she is a girl from a wealthy family, chaperoned by a nurse who is also a confidante. And she is, incredibly enough, to be given in marriage to the mastersinger who, the next morning, sings the best mastersong.

The young man is slightly daunted when he hears this. He hadn't imagined that there would be any such complication when, last night, he arrived as a stranger in Nuremberg, stayed as a guest at her father's house, and promptly fell in love with her. But he is, we soon discover, a knight. The kind that comes in shining armour to rescue maidens in distress – and here is a maiden who has been put in a particularly stressful situation. He hasn't a notion of what a mastersinger is, but he promptly decides to become one and win the girl himself – especially as she has rather boldly said in front of the nurse that she will have 'euch oder keinen' – 'you or no one.'

The nurse, as nurses are wont to do, decides to help. Her name is Magdalene, and she'll ask the young man *she* is in love with, David, to fill the knight in on all the complicated rules that make up the art of mastersinging. As she sighs about her David, David is suddenly there – not much more than a boy, ready to be of service. So the ladies leave, and David, because he loves his Magdalene and will do anything she asks, begins to instruct the knight on what he must know – while a crew of apprentices start merrily rearranging the church pews for the mastersinger meeting that is soon to take place there in the church.

And why should David, who is just an apprentice, know anything about mastersinging? Because, as he announces with great self-importance, his master, the shoemaker Hans Sachs, is Nuremberg's greatest mastersinger. 'Shoemaking and poetry, I'm learning them both together,' he says:

> Schumacherei und Poeterei,
> die lern' ich da alleinerlei.

First of all, David tells the young knight, you've got to master a good hundred tones – that is to say, in today's parlance, a good hundred tunes. Now, I know easily a hundred tunes by Jerome Kern, but I doubt if I could have learned them all in a single night. And David expects the young knight to learn the short tune, the long tune, the overlong tune, the red, the blue, and the green tunes, the nightingale, the goldfinch, the lark, the pelican tunes – and many, many more. But that, he adds, only gets you up to the rank of 'singer.'[12] You have to be able to put words and rhymes of your own to the different tunes before you've advanced to the rank of 'poet.' And then you have to fashion a poem of your own into a song from the various tunes – a song consisting of a *Stollen*, another *Stollen*, and an *Abgesang*. Then and only then you may be judged a master.

Our knight's head is spinning from all the detail,[13] and he hasn't an idea what a *Stollen* and an *Abgesang* might be. (A *Stollen*, after all, is a raisin-filled roll you pick up at the baker's shop.)[14] All the same, he still hopes, rules or no rules, to advance with one great leap to master status that very day, at the meeting there in St Katherine's church.

David wishes him luck, and adds that there will be an official judge, a 'marker,' at the audition, who'll sit in a boxed enclosure (the other apprentices are busy setting it up even then), and this marker will chalk up, on a slate, every violation of the rules. 'Seven mistakes,' warns David, 'are all you are allowed.'

The mastersingers begin to arrive, one by one, two by two, for their meeting. There are in all twelve good burghers from twelve different trades who have advanced to master's standing in singing, and we should note at least four of them. First, Veit Pogner, the goldsmith with the nubile daughter. Second, entering with Pogner, the town clerk, Sixtus Beckmesser, a crotchety fellow who has hopes himself of winning the girl and, as luck would have it, is going to be the marker today. Third, Fritz Kothner, a baker, who will chair the meeting, and is even now calling the roll. (Appropriately, he is the one who will tell us what *Stollen* means outside of the bakery.) And, last to enter, the shoemaker Hans Sachs, almost lost in the group, save that young David impertinently points him out when his name is called.

It is the goldsmith, Pogner, who asks to speak first. 'You know,' he says, 'that tomorrow we are going to cel-ebrate that beautiful feast day, St John the Baptist's day. There'll be parades and games and dancing on the open meadow and, to cap it all, a song competition. Now, God has made me a rich man. I started to think, "What should we put up as a prize?" Well, as often as I've travelled through Germany I've heard people high and low calling us burghers and guild members mere money-grubbers. They don't seem to care that we're the only ones in the whole of Germany who are still interested in art, and in keeping the old traditions alive. I want to show the world that what we really value here in Nuremberg is not money but what is true, good, and beautiful. So, Masters, I propose that, to the master who wins the song contest tomorrow, I shall give, with the rights to all my property, Eva, my only child, in marriage.'

That generous offer brings the other Masters to their feet with shouts of approval, even though most of them are married men already, and thus out of competition. Pogner then adds a crucial proviso: the master they choose must meet with his daughter's approval. All the same, he insists, she can never marry anyone but a master.

Quite a debate begins at that point. Beckmesser is a bachelor, and he is confident that he can win the contest, but not so confident that the girl will want him if he does. So he opposes the proviso. Hans Sachs suggests that, even with the proviso, the offer puts too much strain on the girl: let the decision be subject to the unanimous approval of all the people in Nuremberg as well. That gets all the masters on his back. 'Art will fall into disgrace,' they say, 'if it runs after popularity and courts the favours of the people. *Our* art is judged by its rules alone.'

So Sachs grows bolder and says something very wise: the rules should be tested once a year, and by an outsider, to see if they are really serving their purpose. (The apprentices, eavesdropping on the debate, make merry over that suggestion.)

Beckmesser is callow enough to suggest that Sachs is making an issue because he's a widower and loved by the people and wants the girl for himself. Sachs replies that both he and Beckmesser are in fact too old for the girl. Finally, the twelve masters vote to accept Pogner's generous proposal, with the sole proviso that whoever wins the contest must also be acceptable to the girl.

Now to the next article of business. Does any newcomer seek admission to the mastersingers' guild? Pogner speaks again. 'I'd like to recommend a young knight, Walther von Stolzing, from Franconia. He has just left his castle and all his lands to come and settle with us here in Nuremberg as a burgher, because he loves art and music.'

Our knight steps forward and faces the questions put to him by Kothner, the chairman: 'Who is the master who taught him?'

Walther announces that it was another Walther – the famous minnesinger Walther von der Vogelweide.

'Oh, long since dead,' mutters Beckmesser.

But young Walther goes on to say that he found a book of old Walther's songs in his castle, and read it by his fireside in winter.

'And what was the school in which he learned?'

'The school of the birds in the meadow,' he answers, 'when winter was over and spring came. The songbirds sang just as the book had said to sing' (and rightly so, for Vogelweide in German means 'bird meadow').

'And will his theme now be sacred or secular?'

'What is sacred to me,' Walther exclaims, 'I'll wave love's banner, and sing with my hopes high!'

'We call that secular,' the chairman says, dubiously.[15]

Will Walther get his mastership on the first try? Well, Beckmesser, a kind of poet and pedant overture all by himself, takes his slate and his chalk and gets into the marker's box, and chairman Kothner reads out the most important rules of all. They are inscribed, almost enshrined, on a *Tabulatur*, a lordly plaque that hangs on the church wall, and they are very important for understanding the opera as a whole: a song shall consist of a *Stollen*, or strophe, and then a second *Stollen*, with the same melody and rhyme scheme as the first. And then there must be an *Abgesang*, an 'after-song,' as long as the two *Stollen* together, with a wholly new melody. (Kothner the baker sings out these rules in four Germanic lines of recitative that end with Bach-like falling scales that are lavishly – and hilariously – ornamented.)

Walther, a little intimidated, sits in the ceremonial singer's chair, and starts his trial song. It is a frenzied, undisciplined, ultra-Romantic outpouring about spring sweeping across the earth – like his own passion, of course. And at the end of the first *Stollen*, seven fatal chalk scratches are distinctly heard from the marker's box. Already, it seems, Walther has lost on points. But he rises from his chair and goes on anyway, with an even more furious *Stollen* about winter lying in ambush – like Beckmesser in the marker's box, of course.

When that second *Stollen* is sung, Beckmesser pokes his head out and asks, 'Are you finished?'

'Why do you ask that?' says Walther, who is, at this point, only halfway through his song.

'Because there's no more room on my slate,' shouts Beckmesser, and he shows his slate, simply covered over with chalk marks.

A near-riot breaks out. The masters, unable to make much sense of what seems to them improvised chaos, refuse to hear any more. And Sachs counters, sensibly, 'You're passing judgment on something that does not accord with your rules. You should try to understand *its* rules! Hear him out to the end.' But Sachs is shouted down.

Walther, furious but determined to finish his song, actually stands up on the chair and sings his *Abgesang* over the shouts of the masters – while the apprentices make merry knocking over the furniture. The *Abgesang* is, like the two *Stollen* that preceded it, Walther's imaginative view of the situation there in the church: a golden songbird rises above a crowd of raucous magpies and crows and soars through the air, back to the meadow where the birds sing like Walther von der Vogelweide. When the confusion is over, and the headstrong young

knight has clearly failed his audition, Sachs is left alone in
the church, wondering about the madness of it all. And
there is one strain in Walther's impetuous song he can't
get out of his head – just a transitional strain, a throw-
away. But it's new, it's strangely chromatic, and as he
ponders it, he finds that it is remarkably beautiful:

Let's pause in our story now for a few *obiter dicta*. What
we have here is, uncharacteristically for Wagner, a comedy. But I don't think that it has been remarked very
often how much in the mainstream of comedy it is. Each
one of the characters is, for example, a comic type. I has-
ten to add that each is nicely individualized and three-
dimensional, but fundamentally Walther, Eva, Sachs, and
the others are the stock-in-trade of the comic stage – typical characters. And our situation, charming as it is, had
been seen on the stage hundreds of times before Wagner
put it there. For our long comic tradition in the West goes
back to the Roman comedians Plautus and Terence in the
second century B.C., and before them to the fourth century B.C., to the Athenian Menander and to what is now
called 'New' Comedy. In the fragments of Menander and
in the twenty-six surviving plays of the Romans, we
have, in play after play, these characters:

the inexperienced young hero who has only till morning to win his girl, and who is lectured at from all sides
(the *adolescens* – Wagner's young knight, Walther);

the experienced slave who does most of the lecturing
but gets into a lot of trouble himself (the *servos* – Wagner's apprentice, David);

the girl who is going to be given away in the morning
(the *mulier* – Wagner's Eva);

the nurse or confidante who tries to help the boy get
the girl (the *nutrix* – here, Magdalene);

the philosophizing old man, often secretly in love himself with the girl (the *senex* – Wagner's Hans Sachs, as
we shall soon see);

the procurer who puts the girl up for sale (the *leno* –
considerably softened by Wagner as Eva's father, Pogner);

and the ridiculously over-confident braggart soldier,
who hopes to buy the girl in the morning (the *miles gloriosus*, whom Shakespeare used as a model for Falstaff,
but who appears even more visibly as Wagner's Beckmesser).

I mention all of this, not because I am a professor of
classics, or to imply that Wagner's comedy is unduly
derivative, but to place *Die Meistersinger* where it
deserves to be placed – in the great comic tradition of the

West, from Greek Menander to the Romans Plautus and
Terence, to Renaissance Italy, to Lope de Vega, Shakespeare in *The Tempest*, Molière in *Les Fourberies de Scapin*,
and Beaumarchais, Mozart, and Rossini in the Figaro
plays. All of those post-classical writers use the old plot
and characters. But of all of them Wagner in *Die Meistersinger* has, I think, the characters truest to classic type.
And yet, *mirabile dictu*, they seem perfectly at home transferred to sixteenth-century Germany.

I suspect that Wagner availed himself of the most traditional of plots, with the most typical of characters,
because he wanted a solid base for what was going to be,
on one level, an autobiographical manifesto. In *Die Meistersinger* he casts himself, as in most of his operas, as the
outsider who hopes to find acceptance in a closed society.
So his *adolescens* comes from northern Franconia to
Nuremberg, from a titled estate to a bourgeois society.
We are not told what this young outsider is called till he
sings his trial song – and then the association with the
best German poetic tradition (Walther von der Vogelweide) is nicely established. But the name Walther is
close enough to the name Wagner to suggest an autobiographical identification. And the mastersingers who
oppose Walther are clearly the critics who had opposed
Wagner for some thirty years. Beckmesser (called Veit
Hanslich in the second draft of the libretto) is beyond
much doubt the Viennese music critic Eduard Hanslick.[16]

It is even possible to say, once we've introduced
Hanslick as Beckmesser, that Hans Sachs is intended to
represent Beethoven, whose mantle Wagner claimed and
Hanslick would deny him. But one hesitates to push that

identification too far, for Sachs will also speak, in his great monologues in the acts to come, for the mature Wagner himself. Let us say that Sachs represents the whole German tradition in art and music: the historical Hans Sachs, and Martin Luther, and Bach, and Goethe, and all the famous figures to Beethoven. In the course of the opera, Wagner can, through Sachs, show that German tradition marvelling at and fighting for Wagner/Walther's music as a new and true expression of the best in the past.

One of the many astonishing things about *Die Meistersinger* is how the old Greek and Roman plot blossoms, in Wagner's shaping imagination, into a dramatic and musical structure of cathedralesque proportions, and how eventually it is used to state a kind of artistic creed: that a work of art is made of both youthful ardour (Walther) and mature experience (Hans Sachs), of inspiration (Walther) and hard work (Hans Sachs), of innovating spirit (Walther) and respect for tradition (Hans Sachs). And it must be dedicated to an ideal: it must serve and save the community. But now we're anticipating our story. Let's return to it.

CHAPTER TWO

The Second Stollen

Act II is all elder and linden blossoms,[1] moonlight, and midsummer madness, set in a cobbled street that winds between the slope-roofed houses of old Nuremberg.[2] It is growing dark, and the apprentices are putting up the shutters all through the city. And there's a little malice in their song: on St John's eve, the summer solstice, everyone goes a little mad. Especially when it comes to love: the old man woos the young girl, the young boy woos the old maid. It seems as if all the town is aware that young David is courting old Magdalene and, conversely, that old Sachs has a romantic interest in young Eva. And for the first time, we think: Sachs is a widower and, as the mastersinger of them all, he could easily win the contest. Would Eva have him if he won? Is he interested in her romantically? The plot thickens in Act II.

First, Magdalene scolds young David because his crash course on the rules didn't get Walther through his exam. Then Pogner walks home with his daughter Eva (his fine house is just across the street from Sachs's humbler workshop) and he wonders if he went too far, offering her publicly for a mastersong. Then Sachs sits alone under his elder tree, to enjoy the evening air while working on the shoes he promised Beckmesser in the morning, and the tree, all but become a person, casts a meditative spell over him. He still can't get that strain of Walther's song out of his head – the one that haunted him as the curtain fell on Act I. It followed no rule, but all the same had no fault. In a way it was old, yet it seemed so new, like the song of birds in springtime. How, he wonders, is a man capable of composing something like that? Because, he tells the elder tree, a poet *has* to sing. And because he has to, he can: the 'süsse Not,' the sweet compulsion of spring, prompts a bird to sing, and in the same way the sweet compulsion to create drives a poet to compose. And both the bird and the poet sing beyond any powers they ever knew they had.[3] It's a moment of rare beauty, this 'Fliedermonolog,' this monologue under the elder tree.

Meanwhile, Eva has heard from Magdalene that Walther has failed his audition. As the shadows gather, she comes to Sachs under the elder tree. This is a deli- cately written scene: she wants Sachs to help her and Walther that night while there is still time, but she doesn't know how to say it outright. She talks around the subject, and we discover that, in years past, Sachs has lost, not only his wife, but his children as well. Both he and Eva have thought, separately, about marrying. When she was small, he used to carry her in his arms; now he might take her into his house as both child and wife.[4]

But Sachs suspects from her questions that the man she really loves is not him but Walther. He says he is sorry that the young knight has failed his test; he may already be a master instinctively, but he has shown himself alto- gether too head-strong and self-destructive to be a master as Nuremberg defines the term. Eva quickly reacts to this, and runs off in a huff – a clear indication to Sachs that it is Walther she really loves! 'I thought so,' he says. And though he has, in an outburst of his own, revealed that he envies both Walther's genius and his youth, he adds, 'Well, we must find a way to help the two of them.'

It has grown quite dark now. Sachs closes up his shop, leaving only a crack of candlelight to shine out of his half-door and across the street. And he sees what he thought he would see: Walther and Eva, thoroughly disillusioned with Nuremberg, planning to elope. That would only mean misery for all of them – so he opens the top of his half-door, widening the path of the light, and forces the two young people to retreat into the shadows, under a linden tree. They can't escape up the side street, because, first, the night watchman comes down its slope, sounding his horn to mark the tenth hour, and then Beckmesser appears on its cobblestones, plunking on his lute, eager to try out the mastersong he has prepared for tomorrow morning by using it to serenade Eva at her window tonight. (As it turns out, the one he unwittingly serenades is Magdalene, who is sitting at the window in Eva's clothes, for Eva has put on Magdalene's clothes to elope in.)

It all builds up into a justly famous scene of comic cross-purposes, one in which Eva exclaims, after her scenes with her father, Hans Sachs, Walther, and now Beckmesser, 'What awful trouble I keep having with men!' Sachs, to prevent the elopement, starts hammering away, singing a cobbler's song at the top of his voice. Beckmesser pleads with him to stop. 'You'll wake up the whole neighbourhood ... she's going to think it's *me* singing that!'

'But,' says Sachs, 'I've got to work into the night or I won't have your shoes ready for tomorrow morning. Perhaps we can work something out. You want to try out your song, and I want to finish your shoes. Let me act as a marker for you. I'll hammer away at the shoe whenever you make a slip in your song.'

Beckmesser is anxious to get his new shoes made, and he's also anxious to get a little constructive criticism from the best mastersinger in town, so he starts his serenade, and every time he makes a mistake (and he makes quite a few) Sachs smashes on the shoe.

After two *Stollen*, Sachs asks, 'Are you finished?'

'Why do you ask that?' says Beckmesser who is, of course, only half-way through his song.

'Because I'm finished with the shoes,' says Sachs, and he shows the soles, simply studded with hammered nails.

Beckmesser furiously starts his *Abgesang* anyway, and soon the whole neighbourhood *is* awakened ... and sweaty nightcaps aren't all that come down from the second-storey windows. Act II ends, as Act I did, with an *Abgesang* shouted out over protests, and then with a full-scale brawl: all the guilds are going at it – tinkers, tailors, weavers, tanners, apprentices, journeymen, and even masters – and Beckmesser is set upon by David, who is furious when he sees him serenading his Magdalene. Sachs manages to stop the elopers, pushing Eva into her house, and pulling Walther with him into his. And suddenly they all scatter, as Germans are wont to do, before the voice of authority: the night watchman comes doddering around the corner again, and finds the street as peaceful as can be. It is as if there has been no disturbance at all. He sounds his horn, the music goes all elder and linden blossoms, and the moon rises on the empty cobbled street.

Let's pause again for a few more *obiter dicta*: something about *Stollen* and *Abgesang*. By now we've heard a lot about how a mastersong is properly constructed. In Act I David told us there had to be two *Stollen*, or stanzas, of identical length, each a variation on the same melody, with a rhyme at the end. And then, as a kind of resolution, there had to be an *Abgesang*, an aftersong, as long as the two *Stollen* together, with a melody of its own.

Then, when Walther introduced himself to the master's guild, he had the rules on his mind, and – though I didn't mention this in my run through the plot – his biographical remarks, about reading the poems of Walther von der Vogelweide by his fireside and then learning from the meadow birds themselves, actually took the form of a mastersong: two matching *Stollen* and an *Abgesang*. One of the masters, Kunz Vogelgesang, even spotted that, and liked what he heard, but Beckmesser shouted him down. (Meanwhile, Wagner has subtly made the point that his Walther is instinctively a master already.)

Then Kothner read out the rules about two *Stollen* and an *Abgesang* from the *Tabulatur* on the wall, and Walther began his trial song – a not-too-perfect specimen of a mastersong, as Walther got terribly excited and allowed his two *Stollen* to run on too long, and his *Abgesang* was hardly audible above the shouts of the outraged masters.

Now, in Act II, we've had Beckmesser's serenade – not too bad actually, in terms of two matching *Stollen* and resolving *Abgesang*, but it was a painfully literal application of the rules, and Beckmesser has a terrible tendency to put the accént on the wrong sylláble. By now, we're fairly adept ourselves at these judgments; we've had instructions from David and Kothner, two examples from Walther, and one from Beckmesser.

And why do we feel, instinctively, that every note and every bar of this long opera is exactly in place? Well, some seventy years ago, Albert Lorenz, in an exhaustive analysis of Wagner's operas called *Das Geheimnis der Form bei Richard Wagner*, demonstrated that, if you consider the overture as a separate piece, Act I and Act II of *Die Meistersinger* are approximately the same length, that there are a dozen or so incidents, and even some bits of dialogue, in Act I that are paralleled in Act II, and that each act ends with a sort of rhyme in the story – public rioting over what is judged bad singing.

In other words, Acts I and II are two *Stollen*. And Act III is an *Abgesang*: as long as Acts I and II together, with a new strain of seriousness and purposefulness, effecting a harmonious solution of all the conflicts in Acts I and II. The whole opera, then, can be said to be one immense mastersong. The whole of *Meistersinger* is Wagner's answer to his critics, a song offered to them to meet *their* specifications, marvellously replete with all the things *they* demanded from and found wanting in his other work – diatonic structures, counterpoint, singable tunes, duets, ensembles, folk dances worthy of Weber and chorales worthy of Bach, delicate genre scenes, and, above all, thoroughly human characters.

And that, I suppose, is why this is the least of Wagner's works for some Wagnerites: it is too far removed from the seething chromaticism of *Tristan*, the powerful subconscious world of the *Ring*, and the mysticism and transparently lovely musical textures of *Parsifal*. For perfect Wagnerites, *Die Meistersinger* is merely Wagner returning to a subject that had amused him many years before, expanding it to demonstrate his skill at handling the well-made play and the trappings of traditional opera, aiming at and winning popularity, silencing his critics, and all the time clearly enjoying himself. But it is not, for them, an essential work.

I can't agree that that is all there is to *Die Meistersinger*. Not once I'm into the *Abgesang*, Act III. There I find Wagner operating at the height of his powers and dealing with issues as profound as those in any of the other works. Actually they are much the same issues – renouncing one's own will and learning compassion. Wagner's critics are quick to point out that those are the very qualities Wagner most conspicuously lacked. But that, it seems to me, is why he wrote works about them – out of the abundance of his genius and the abyss of his own personal need. As Hans Sachs says about the bird in springtime, a sweet compulsion put it in his breast to sing a song he didn't know he knew. To those who ask, 'How could Wagner write of what he didn't know or feel?' Hans Sachs answers, about the bird in springtime,

> sang er, wie er musst'
> und wie er musst', so konnt' er's!

Wagner sang about renunciation and compassion 'because he had to ... and, because he had to, he could.'

There is no question that Wagner was the most ambivalent of the great composers. In a many-sided genius, which he was, it is easy to find faults – self-destructive faults – that we ordinary people do not have. That is one of the reasons why the works such geniuses produce are so rich. Artists who cannot work out the problems of their lives are compelled to find solutions in their art. The healthiness, good humour, wisdom, and warm humanity in *Die Meistersinger* – those are precisely what are most missing in Wagner's personal life, and in almost all of his voluminous prose writing. But what he couldn't achieve in his life he did achieve in his art. He had to, and because he had to, he was able to.

I don't doubt that a good man can produce great art. But more often it is a profoundly ambivalent man who produces the greatest art. When the writer Eduard Schuré met Wagner in 1865, during the composition of *Die Meistersinger*, he exclaimed over 'this ravaged face [that] bore the traces of passions and sufferings capable of wearing down the lives of many men,' this face in which he could see 'both Faust and Mephistopheles, the former viewed from the front, the latter in profile.'[5] When Wagner's second wife, Cosima, saw the tears in his eyes after a performance of *Die Meistersinger*, she wrote, reflecting his own sentiments, 'When future generations seek refreshment in this unique work, may they spare a thought for the tears from which its smiles arose.'[6]

An artist has to pay for the gift of his genius. Wagner paid. He was defeated, one way or another, all his life. His own self-destructiveness always pursued him. There wasn't one of his triumphs that was not spoiled, at the moment of triumph, by his own self-destructiveness. But what *he* couldn't do, his characters do. In his operas, he splits his many-faceted self into those characters. He drains off the evil in himself and, as the long dramas move towards their great catharses, he brings the good together. Hans Sachs does what Wagner wanted to do but never could – renounce his own wilfulness and open up in understanding and compassion to others.

Wagner wrote opera after opera about himself, and that for many makes him an artist of lesser stature. In the greatest art, they say, we are in touch with more than a single individual. We feel the needs and hopes and dreams of all humanity. I submit that Wagner, not in spite of but because of his failed human nature, expresses humanity's needs and hopes more compellingly than any other composer for the stage. We shall see that in Act III of *Die Meistersinger.*

CHAPTER THREE

The Abgesang

Act III of *Die Meistersinger*, the longest act in Wagner, is the *Abgesang*, or aftersong, in which the serious elements in the comedy, only hinted at in the two *Stollen* that preceded it, darken and deepen both text and music.

The act begins with a prelude that verges on the tragic. A solemn, searching theme sounds in the orchestra. Critics have rightly called it the Renunciation Theme:

We have heard it before, half-submerged in the orchestra, in Act II, when Sachs sang his cobbling song to prevent Eva and Walther from eloping. But so much was going on in that scene that we might have missed it there. Sachs was tapping away at Beckmesser's shoe, singing at the top of his voice to Eva, fully aware that she was hiding in the shadows with Walther and waiting for the chance to run away with him. Sachs knew that, one way or another, he was going to lose her, and his sadness welled up, not in the accompaniment to the song, not in the song itself, but – if I may put it this way – in the song within the song. Eva said to Walther in the shadows, 'That song brings me pain. I don't know why.' Why should the jolly cobbler tune with the jauntily ironic words have caused her pain that she cannot explain? It was the song within the song, the Renunciation Theme, barely audible but almost tangible, that moved her, that made her exclaim, 'Oh, dearest of men, what sorrow I have brought to you!'

I'd like to encourage you, when next you listen to *Die Meistersinger*, to listen especially for the song within the song, the tears within the laughter, in Act III. Wagner himself encourages us to see Act III this way, by stating the once-hidden theme clearly and solemnly, on the cellos, as the act begins.

The prelude continues, slowly pondering two more themes – the cobbling song, in which new depths are now revealed, and the 'Wach auf!' chorus that will greet Sachs in the opera's final scene, now intoned with great tenderness on the French horns. At the start of these considerations I remarked that, among the many themes that jostle one another in the prelude to Act I there was, strangely, no theme that referred to Hans Sachs. The prelude to Act III is that earlier prelude's counterpart and its emotional completion. It is the musical portrait of Hans Sachs we have been waiting for. It is as if we are seeing at last into his soul.

When the curtain rises, the first rays of morning are streaming through the window of Sachs's workshop, and we see him sitting at his desk, bent over a book, totally absorbed.[1] We are about to begin the long, marvellous scene wherein all the major characters come to see him privately, and all their various problems begin, under his benign guidance, to solve themselves.

First is David, who apologizes for his midsummer madness – pummelling away at Beckmesser – the night before.[2] He gets his daily singing lesson, and in the course of singing about John the Baptist he remembers, of a sudden, that this day, Johannistag, is also the name day of his master, Hans. The apprentice congratulates his master, and is bold enough to say what many people around Nuremberg are saying – that Hans Sachs could, and should, enter the song contest and make Eva, whom he has always loved, his wife.

Then Sachs sits alone in thought, framed in his window, bent again over his book. And Wagner's omniscient orchestra seems to speak to him. It says again what it said in the midst of his Act II cobbler song. Eva heard it speak then, and so, if we were listening closely, did we. Now that Renunciation Theme sounds clearly, slowly, and Sachs, following the lead of the orchestra, takes it up. He knows that he must renounce his dream of marrying Eva, having children again, and finding happiness. And at every important moment in Act III, with every deeper realization that Sachs must renounce his own will to marry Eva, the theme will rise in the orchestra.

Renouncing one's will is one of Wagner's perennial themes. He found it most persuasively expressed in Arthur Schopenhauer's intensely pessimistic treatise *The World as Will and Representation*, which he first read in 1854, when he was writing *Die Walküre*, and to which he returned many times when writing the rest of the *Ring*, *Tristan*, *Die Meistersinger*, and *Parsifal*. For Schopenhauer the fundamental reality in the universe was a blind, undifferentiated power that he called *Wille* (will). It operates in nature as gravity and other physical forces, in animals as instinct, and in humans as an insatiable passion that drives us through lives of endless illusion, unfulfilment, and suffering. That destructive force within us, Schopenhauer said, must be consciously acknowledged, renounced, and overcome. In *Die Meistersinger*, Wagner refers to it, not as *Wille*, the usual Schopenhauer term, but – in another of the philosopher's words, one for which there is no exact English equivalent – as *Wahn*. 'Madness' is the usual translation, or 'illusion' or even 'delusion.' Perhaps Wagner chose *Wahn* rather than *Wille* for use in *Die Meistersinger* because in one of its senses *Wahn* can be thought a proper concern of comedy, which sets out to correct the madness and dispel the illusions that beset and delude humankind. But other, deeper meanings of *Wahn* soon come into play.

Looking up from his book – which, we discover, is a history of the world – Sachs sings his greatest monologue: 'Wahn, Wahn, überall Wahn' – 'Madness, madness, everywhere madness.' Why, he wonders, 'do we hurt one another? Why do we hurt ourselves? We dig into our own flesh, and cannot even hear our cry of pain.'[3] Destruction and self-destruction – it goes on and on, everywhere, this *Wahn*. It is ingrained, a part of us, instinctive and irrational. It seems from all my reading that nothing happens in human lives without it. No one escapes it, least of all me.'

Wagner knew all too well of the self-destructive streak within him, the mad streak, that, as Robert Donington once put it, 'runs through human nature like some tragic flaw in bright metal.'[4] He builds his music to a frighteningly abrupt climax, and then his Hans Sachs rises from his book, goes to his window, and looks out on the dawn rising over his Nuremberg, still slumbering in the heart of Germany. The music rises proudly and nobly, and – Wagner says in his stage directions – Sachs is filled with a deep, quiet joy. The realization comes to him that he need not despair of human nature. Last night, partly at his own instigation, the whole city was filled with madness. 'God only knows how it happened. Was it the spirits that appear on St John's Eve?' The music softens to dreamlike textures as he wonders about an illusory desire he himself felt last night: 'Was it a midsummer glowworm looking for a mate? Was it the scent of the elder tree? In any case, that was St John's Eve. Madness and strange spirits were on the loose. But now we have' (and the orchestra rises in an outpouring of song) 'St John's Day.'

What that orchestral sunburst means is that, watching the light break over his beloved city, Sachs has seen – and in a moment he will tell us he has seen – that *Wahn*, irrational and ineradicable as it may be, need not be altogether destructive. The irrational – what psychologists were to call, soon after Wagner, the unconscious – is a part of us that we ignore at our peril, for it lies deep within us and has the power to destroy us. Yet, strangely, it is through the same irrational element in human nature that works of art are produced.[5] It can be either our weakness or our strength.

While composing *Die Meistersinger* Wagner wrote an essay explaining the positive aspects of *Wahn*.[6] Eventually he named the home he built at Bayreuth Wahnfried – the place where his *Wahn* found peace, even as Hans Sachs in his workshop found peace in acknowledging the potential destructiveness in human nature and carrying on all the same, finding strength in human weakness, making good things out of what, for better or worse, he was. In the rest of the act Sachs will act accordingly, expressing sympathy for the sufferings of others and helping them as best he can – strong recommendations from Schopenhauer himself. Sachs ends his long meditation saying, 'If nothing ever happens in our lives without a touch of *Wahn*, let us see if we cannot put *Wahn* to work for us, to accomplish some noble end here in Nuremberg.' The orchestra hints that he may have already thought of a way in which Walther, though disqualified from the song contest, will be able to enter it and win the hand of Eva.

Walther is the second character to visit Sachs in his workshop. He has had 'a little sleep, but good and sound' – 'ein wenig, aber fest und gut.' He has also had 'a wonderfully beautiful dream.'

'Ah,' says Sachs, 'man's truest *Wahn* is revealed to him in his dreams. You know, my son, all of art and poetry is nothing but the interpretation of dreams.[7] It is very likely that your dream told you how to become a master this very day.'

In fact, Walther has heard a song in his dream! He scarcely dares to think of it now, for fear that it will fade away. Sachs, excited, suggests that they write it down and make it conform to the mastersinger's rules.

'Why do we need the rules?' Walther asks, with the usual impatience of the young and the headstrong. And Sachs answers: 'In the sweet time of youth, anyone can write a song – their springtime sings *for* them. But then come a man's summer, and autumn, and winter. Births and deaths, sorrows and joys. Then only a few can sing beautiful songs – only those who have learned the rules.' He wisely cautions the young genius that tradition is not a dead weight to be thrown off and cast aside, but a heritage of wisdom and experience that, rightly used, nourishes a new artist in the act of creation. It is a lesson that

Wagner himself learned only gradually. 'Rules,' says Sachs, 'enable poets to capture again their intuitive visions, and make works of art out of them. Follow the rules now, and your dream will become a song.'

So Walther sings, and Sachs writes down the words, and in the workshop where shoes are usually made we see a song fashioned. It is a wonderful scene. A work of art is created before our very eyes and ears – a *Stollen* first, then a matching *Stollen* to the same melody, then an *Abgesang*, twice as long, with a beautiful new melody and a resolution. And the words? They describe a dream-like morning vision of a woman standing beneath the Tree of Life. Sachs is deeply moved as he bends over his desk, writing the song down, and the Renunciation Theme sounds briefly in the orchestra: it is clear that this morning Walther, not he, will win the contest, and marry Eva.

The song is complete, and still the words come pouring out of Walther: a whole new set – another pair of *Stollen* and another *Abgesang*. Now the words describe an evening vision of a woman beneath a laurel tree, her eyes lit like distant stars. Sachs, lifting his pen from his paper, is again deeply moved, and the Renunciation Theme sounds again, more beautifully harmonized.

Sachs encourages Walther to go on: 'Tell us what these dream visions mean.' But Walther, an intuitive genius, is too impatient with structural matters to compose any more. Sachs lets him go. He is content. He has the words down – more than enough, he knows, to win Eva for Walther if only, somehow, he can find a way to get the disqualified Walther back into the contest. He takes the young man upstairs, where they will don their best clothes for the great event.

The next to call in at the workshop is Beckmesser, still limping from the beating he got from David in the brawl the night before.[8] He finds the shop empty, spots the new song ink-fresh on the desk and, thinking it is by Sachs, pockets it instantly. Sachs comes in, dressed now for the festival day, sizes up the situation, and makes Beckmesser a present of the song. He decides to let Beckmesser be his own undoing. He knows that this pedant who knows only rules will come to grief attempting to sing a song that came out of a dream.

Beckmesser leaves the workshop triumphantly waving the words of the song he is sure will enable him to win the contest and the girl, and there is another caller at Sachs's door – that young girl, Eva, radiant in a white wedding dress, but complaining that the new shoes Sachs made for her for this day of days do not fit.[9] Sachs stoops to examine them, does some professional readjusting, and there is, at this lowly moment, a *coup de théâtre*. Walther appears in the doorway, clad now as if in shining armor, come to rescue the maiden, come to sing what he couldn't sing a few minutes before – the meaning of his midsummer night's dream: the two women in the previous versions of the song have now come together in the one beautiful woman he sees standing before him. Eva is the fulfilment of the morning and evening visions he has seen in his dream.

Suddenly we have, for many, the great moment in the drama. The Renunciation Theme sounds with an almost tragic savagery. Sachs is kneeling at Eva's feet, still busy

with her shoe. She, overwhelmed by the song her knight
has composed for her, knowing now that everything will
turn out all right for them, bursts into tears of commin-
gled joy and sorrow. The moment has finally come for
Sachs: he must surrender Eva to the young man she
loves. She clings to Sachs, still the little girl that he has
loved, and he tenderly draws away, and places her in
Walther's arms. Then for a moment, he almost despairs.
Is there anything left for him in life? Irrationally, he lashes
out at David and Walther and Beckmesser and Eva, who
have all come to him that morning. He sees them now as
the destroyers of his happiness. For a moment, it is as if
the wise Sachs is lost to *Wahn*, close to despair, unable to
face yet another wrenching loss in his life. The moment is
'the most piercing in the opera, and certainly the most
Schopenhauerian.'[10] Then Eva turns to him, and sings,
just this once, with the surging power of an Isolde: 'O
Sachs, my friend, you dear man. How can I ever thank
you? Without you I would have remained always a child.
But you taught me to think and to feel. You made me
blossom ...'

Then the omniscient orchestra quotes the yearning
theme from Wagner's *Tristan*, and Sachs sings, over that
famously chromatic music, 'My child, I know a sad story
about Tristan and Isolde. I don't want to play the part of
King Marke.' He knows that Eva was meant for Walther,
that he must not come between them. And the music
resignedly works its way back from *Tristan*'s chromaticism to the solid diatonic tonality of *Die Meistersinger*.[11]

Then there is a final caller at the door – Magdalene,
come to accompany her David to the songfest. So Sachs

has two pairs of lovers to assist him in naming, according to the masters' practice, the new-born song. Do you remember all those songs that David listed in Act I, the tunes that past mastersingers had written? Some of them had outlandish names, like 'The Cinnamonstick Melody.' David playfully said that when he didn't learn his lesson Sachs made him sing the 'Knieriem-Schlag-Weis' ('The Strap on the Knee Melody') and Magdalene made him sing the 'Eitel Brot-und-Wasser-Weis,' ('The Plain Bread and Water Melody'). Well, Walter's new song is christened the 'Selige Morgentraum-Deut-Weise.' It's a pretty big name for an infant song: 'The Meaning of the Blessed Morning-Dream Melody.'

Sachs charmingly turns the event into a baptism. And so that David can be a proper sponsor at the ceremony, Sachs has him kneel for a cuff on the ear: the apprentice is thereby made a journeyman, and can marry his Magdalene. And all five of them sing of their happiness, with musical strands of the new song threaded radiantly through their quintet. The music is not far from tears, nor are we – not sentimental tears, but tears of joy that art can reconcile, unite, and bring beauty, happiness, and peace.

I am more moved by *Die Meistersinger* than by any other opera because Sachs is what I would like to be. He is an educator who teaches not just rules and techniques but how to think and how to feel. He loves music as much as he loves his chosen profession, and he sees the connection between the two. He is, at least at the time the opera takes place, a celibate whose only children are those whose lives he touches and enriches. He is the good man who generously helps Walther to shape his intuitive inspirations, who wisely guides Eva in her unfolding love for Walther, who teaches David his trade while at the same time opening him up to wider issues, and who opposes Beckmesser because Beckmesser can destroy the happiness of the others – and besides, Beckmesser too has a lot to learn.

But Sachs – like the Marschallin in Richard Strauss's *Der Rosenkavalier*, a figure clearly patterned after him – Sachs also learns. He comes to see deeply into life, to accept its inevitable limitations, and to embrace it fully. And that acceptance brings a profound reward in terms of growth of character and spiritual insight. Sachs is the character in all opera that a man, when he doubts and fails and prays and wonders about the meaning of life, can most identify with, and grow with. At least, I do.[12]

So we move to the song contest on grassy banks of the river Pegnitz, the scene Germans call the *Festwiese*, the 'festival in the meadow.' I can't think of a more jubilant scene in all of opera. The whole town of Nuremberg is there – its guilds, its toy makers, its marching trumpeters and drummers, and, in procession, its mastersingers. And as the music rises to a great climax, all of them join together to surprise Hans Sachs on his arrival by singing a tribute to him:

> Awake! The day is dawning.
> I hear a joyous nightingale
> singing in the greenwood.
> His song rings out through mountain and valley.
> Night is sinking in the west
> and day is rising in the east.

The russet glow of morning
is sending rays through the troubled clouds ...

Those are words that the historical Hans Sachs once wrote in honour of Martin Luther. Now they are sung in honour of Sachs himself. It should be a moment of great joy for him, but the Renunciation Theme enters to colour the final cadence of the chorale: at the moment he is hailed by the people as the herald of a new age of artistic achievement, Sachs remembers that, in his private life, he has already surrendered his beloved to, and passed his insights on to, a younger man.

In a moving speech, he tells the crowd that they honour him too much, that it is not he, but Eva's father, Pogner, who, with his generous offer, has shown real faith in art.

But Pogner's heart is heavy as Beckmesser mounts the podium. Will he have to give his daughter to that dis-agreeable chap? No, as it turns out. Beckmesser, clutching his lute and shaky in his new shoes, has difficulty even standing straight. Then he tries to fit Walther's poem to the tune of his serenade, gets it all laughably wrong, and leaves in a huff, proclaiming, as he thinks is true, that it was Sachs who wrote the horrible jibberish he has tried to sing.

Everyone agrees that the song is a mess, but Sachs claims that it is actually beautiful when properly sung. And, seeing as he stands charged with incompetence before them all, he calls for a witness to the truth of what he says. Can the real author of the song prove him inno-cent? So Walther is after all able to sing, even though he has been disqualified: Walther steps forward, not as a contestant, but as a witness for the defence – and the crowd listens to the song in wondering silence. And so do we, for Walther dares, at this moment of truth, to improvise. He compresses the three former versions of the song into one, so that the whole first version now becomes a *Stollen*, and the second version a *Stollen*, and the third an *Abgesang*! Walther really shouldn't do this, as it is the song as composed in the cobbler's shop, the song Beckmesser couldn't sing right, that is on trial – and chairman Kothner has the page with the words right there at the contest. But Walther's improvisation is so beautiful that Kothner, entranced, drops the page and gazes on the singer. Soon all the people are shouting, though Walther is not even a contestant, 'Give *him* the prize!'

So what Sachs wanted at the start actually happens: the people have a say in the judgment of a work of art. And of course, Eva accepts their verdict. How can she not? She loves the singer of the song.

The opera should be over, and in the opera house all of us are reaching for our hats ... when, unexpectedly, Walther refuses to accept the master's title he has just won. He will have nothing to do with the masters who, the day before, so peremptorily rejected him. In consternation, everyone turns to Sachs. And Sachs sings his last great solo, addressing it to Walther: 'Don't scorn the masters! Honour their art! You owe your success, not to your ancestors, or coat of arms, or spear, or sword, but to the fact that you are a poet – and for that you must thank these bourgeois mastersingers. For all their faults, they alone have kept poetry alive when the rest of Germany, princes and knights included, had neglected it. So I say to you, honour your German masters! For without tradition, without art, no nation can hope to survive.'[13]

The music of the overture returns, and Walther accepts his mastership. But the final praises of the people are bestowed on their beloved Hans Sachs. And rightly so, for not only has he spoken eloquently about the importance of art in a nation's life, he has shown us who have travelled with him through this last act that to give life lovingly is to receive it and to be made whole.

As the music from the overture moves towards its familiar conclusion, Sachs leaves centre stage to Walther and Eva, and is congratulating Pogner on the day's happy outcome. Then we see Eva whisper to Walther; he nods, takes the victor's laurel from his own head, hands it to her, and she walks quietly up behind Sachs and happily circles his head with the prize that he, more than anyone, has won.

In the theatre, we leap to our feet as the curtain falls, grateful if we have seen a good performance, but also proud to the point of cheering that humankind can triumph over madness and produce out of its sorrows great, laughing works of art. I can remember leaving performances of other Wagner operas – *Lohengrin* and *Tristan* and *Parsifal* – walking on air, and turned wonderingly inward. But after *Die Meistersinger*, filled with at least as much emotion, I am turned outwards. I want to embrace all the world. I can remember, as I left the theatre, how Mannheim or Munich, Dortmund or Darmstadt, London or New York or San Francisco seemed transformed – and not just by some midsummer moon or midwinter snow. There was something essentially right with the world.

Life made sense. It was, in fact, full of meaning, and I was eager to live it.

I would like, finally, to speak about one last remarkable feature in this opera. Metaphor. How this work of art radiates meaning on meaning outwards. Just about everything in *Die Meistersinger*, large and small, means something else. And one of the pleasures of hearing it again and again is the thrill of discovering what else and what else and what else it all means.[14]

Gradually, as you listen to *Die Meistersinger*, you become conscious of an almost continuous use of image patterns – words and figures meeting and mating in the text almost as the leitmotifs recur in the music. Consider the various references to songbirds. Walther is first told he must learn such mastersinger tunes as the 'goldfinch,' the 'lark,' and the 'pelican.' But he has his own way of singing, which he learned in winter, by the fireside, from an old book by the famous medieval Walther whose name means 'bird meadow,' and then in the springtime from the meadow birds themselves. He is impatient with the masters, though they bear such names as Konrad Nachtigall (nightingale) and Kunz Vogelgesang (bird song). Even the one who is sick and cannot be there is named Niklaus Vogel (Nicholas Bird). When he sings his trial song, Walther likens himself to a golden bird that soars over hooting owls, rooks, magpies, and crows. No wonder the masters reject him! They know something about metaphor too.

Then in Act II, when, under the elder tree, Sachs reflects how a bird sings instinctively and 'because he must,' he adds, 'There was a nicely shaped beak on that songbird that sang today!' Similarly in Act III, when Sachs tells Walther that his squire has traced him to Nuremberg and brought him his shining armour, he adds, 'It must have been a little dove that told him where his master's nest was.'[15]

And so the bird references continue to the last scene, when all of Nuremberg rises to greet Sachs with that chorale about a nightingale heralding a new dawn. The historical Sachs wrote the words about Martin Luther,[16] but such is the cumulative association of images in the opera that, when we hear the words in Act III, we think, 'Yes, the nightingale in the words is Luther, but Wagner makes the music sound like Bach, and the rising scales in it remind me of John the Baptist, from whose hymn the notes were named, and the people clearly intend the nightingale to represent Hans Sachs, and Hans Sachs himself probably thinks by now that the nightingale is really Walther, and all of us who know the opera think at this point, 'Oh, the nightingale is surely Wagner!' Six dawn-heralding nightingales! Such are the uses of metaphor. Meaning on meaning.

Then throughout the text there are scores of references, literal and metaphorical, to shoes and boots, wax and pitch, leather and last. Well-made songs are, we soon gather, like well-made shoes. Young David, learning the cobbler's trade from Sachs, is at the same time learning about song, and the language of the trade is constantly transferred to the art.

'Schumacherei und Poeterei.' Songs are like shoes. Consider that metaphor working in these situations:

Sachs hammers away at Beckmesser's shoe whenever he finds a fault in his song. Eva insists that her new shoes pinch – but what she wants is not a well-made shoe but a well-made song for her Walther to sing, and while Sachs is busy working on the shoe, Walther appears in the doorway to sing the song. Finally, at the singing contest, Beckmesser, limping in his new shoes and unsure of his footing on the platform, attempts to fit Walther's words to his own melody, with laughable results: neither the shoe nor the song fits.

But we can go deeper. John the Baptist, who presides over this opera, is a figure for Hans Sachs. All of the action takes place on the eve and feast of the saint, but it isn't until Act III that the identification of baptist and shoemaker is fully established. There David, singing about St John, remembers, 'Master ... it's *your* name day.' After that, the identification of saint John and cobbler John really takes hold: Hans Sachs baptizes Walther's newborn song. And the redemptive power of the song, its sacramental grace if you will, goes to work instantly. All of those present find their lives are touched by the song: David is freed from his apprenticeship and given to Magdalene, Eva and Walther know now that they too can marry, and Sachs sees some meaning in his loss of Eva – all of which changes in their lives they promptly sing of in the Quintet. And eventually, on the river bank in the last scene, the sacramental song touches everyone in Nuremberg.

In other words, *Die Meistersinger*, like all of Wagner's operas, is about redemption. We should have known this, really, from the very moment the curtain first went up,

from the words of the hymn the people of Nuremberg
were singing to St John the Baptist:

> Once our Savior came to thee,
> By thy hand baptized to be ...
> Baptist let us share thy rite,
> And be sinless in his sight.
>   Baptist, teacher, Christ's first preacher,
>   Take us by the hand, there on Jordan's strand.

On the surface, this is conventional piety, appropriate to
Reformation Germany. But in the context of the opera, it
works metaphorically too. It is a prayer that Walther may
come to Sachs and be baptized, and that Sachs may teach
his people and lift them up, at their own river, to a true
appreciation of art, to a whole new testament of song.
These worshippers are passionately devoted to art, but,
like the characters in any comedy since Menander, they
need correcting or, to use Wagner's word for it, redeeming. Their cultural leaders are altogether too hidebound
by conventional rules; one of their most eminent citizens
fears that they may have become more interested in
money than in art. And they are named for scriptural sinners who need redeeming – Eve and David and Mary
Magdalen. Like their prototypes in the Bible, David and
Magdalene yearn ardently for redemption – from a long
apprenticeship, so they can marry at last. And Eva must
be saved from Beckmesser, the devil of this piece, surely:
his shoes are finished with pitch, not wax, and he
exclaims 'zum Teufel' ('the devil') at every turn.

Wagner doesn't press all this as far as he might have. He

doesn't name the young hero whose song brings redemption Jesus. After all, the biblical John the Baptist said of Jesus, 'The strap of *His* sandal I am not worthy to loose.' But Walther *is* associated in the text with biblical forerunners and types of Jesus: Eva says at the beginning of the opera that he looks like Dürer's young David attacking Goliath with his sling, and at the end of the opera he accepts membership in the masters' guild with a medallion bearing the image of King David with his harp.

But first and foremost, Walther is associated with Adam. Read the words of Sachs's cobbling song in Act II.[17] Walther and Eva plan to elope, and Sachs tries to stop them with a song, and Beckmesser comes along too with a song. And what does Sachs sing? That when Adam and Eve left paradise they hurt their feet on the gravel outside, and God felt sorry for them and ordered an angel to make them shoes before the devil got the idea he could try his hand at shoemaking. 'Who's he making sport of?' asks Walther, hiding in the shadows with Eva. 'Us or Beckmesser?' Eva, who knows something about metaphor, says, 'He's getting at all three of us!' All four of them, in fact, if you think of Walther as Adam, Eva as Eve, Beckmesser as the devil, and Sachs as the angel barring the way in and out of Paradise. And if you're aware that, in this opera, shoes also mean songs.

Read, too, the words of all the various drafts of our Adam's prize song.[18] First, it is sacred in subject; it draws on the first pages of the Bible – a morning of wonderful light, a garden, a tree branching out over all the others – the Tree of Life itself – and a beautiful woman offering its fruit. In his final version of the song, Walther says it

plainly: This is 'Eve in the Garden of Eden.' 'Eva im
Paradies.'

Then the song becomes secular; it is about art – an
evening when the urge to create is irresistible, a singing
brook, a laurel tree, a woman peering through the
branches. In his final version, Walther says, directly: This
is 'the Muse of Mount Parnassus.' 'Die Muse des Parnass.' He even sings of that Muse baptizing him in the
stream there.

Poor baffled Beckmesser, finding the rough draft, asks,
'Is this a biblical song?' and Sachs replies, rightly, 'You're
missing a lot if you think just that.' Nothing in *Die Meistersinger* works on one level alone. Walther sings a third
version to Eva in her wedding dress, with words that call
to mind German medieval and baroque representations
of the Virgin Mary, with stars circling her head, born in
grace ('Huld-geboren'), chosen as in a Magnificat
('Ruhm-erkoren'). In the Middle Ages they loved to sing
how the 'Ave' in Ave Maria was the reverse of 'Eva' – that
is, how Mary, when she accepted the message of the
angel, reversed the destructive pattern begun by Eve and
began the whole process of redemption. They called
Mary the new Eve because through her came, finally, a
redeeming from the original sin that fatally flawed
humankind – that flaw in our nature that is, in virtually
all mythologies, the dawning awareness of our potential
for good or evil.

So now we come to the heart of *Die Meistersinger*. Now
we can see why baptism is so central a symbol in it. Baptism saves us from the evil effects of original sin, and
gives us grace to help us overcome the defect in our

nature that Hans Sachs calls *Wahn* – that destructive
streak, that mad streak that 'runs through human nature
like some tragic flaw in bright metal.'[19]

Can this really be said of an opera written by that terrible man, Richard Wagner? The Virgin Mary in an opera
by Wagner? It is not as unlikely as might at first appear.
The Virgin Mary was a powerful force in Wagner's earlier
Tannhäuser. And a pervasive motif in all of Wagner's
mature works is what Goethe first called 'das Ewig-weib-
liche,' the eternal feminine that inspires a man and leads
him upwards – redeems him, to use Wagner's term.[20] The
crowning image of Goethe's eternal feminine, on the last,
upwardly spiralling page of his *Faust*, is a vision of the
Virgin Mary. Further, Wagner tells us in his autobiography that it was seeing Titian's massive painting of the
Assumption of the Virgin in Venice that spurred him on
to begin work on the music for *Die Meistersinger* after the
text had lain untended to for many years.[21] (Even he did
not see at once everything there was in this many-splendoured opera.)[22]

As Wagner composed his greatest works, he came
again and again to the same profound realization: the
flaw in our nature, the irrational, potentially destructive
force within us can also be powerfully creative. But it
has to be directed. It has to be, in the context of this
opera, baptized. It has to be, to use Wagner's own term,
redeemed. And the great value of art, which itself arises
out of that basic human drive, is that it can meet that inner
compulsion to destroy, and release its potential to heal
and create.

So *Die Meistersinger*, like all of Wagner's operas, is in

the last analysis a parable of redemption. And what a cleansing baptism that last scene is! Through the song that came out of *Wahn* and was dutifully baptized, the people of Nuremberg are strengthened in their national identity; the mastersingers are freed from the bonds of convention; David is released from his apprenticeship and united with Magdalene; Eva, much to Pogner's relief, is given to her beloved; Walther learns to respect tradition and discipline his art; Beckmesser is chastened (and, we may hope, has learned from the experience); and Sachs, who had grieved at having to give up Eva and had almost despaired of human nature, comes to see that love is given to us to help us in the healing of humanity. The madness, the *Wahn*, that infected the community on St John's Eve is washed away on the river bank on St John's Day. We the audience rise from the long opera cleansed, baptized, full of happiness. And the songbook that is *Die Meistersinger* turns its last shining page.

CHAPTER FOUR

Controversies

W e now have to deal with two problems that in the last decade and a half have come increasingly to dominate discussions of *Die Meistersinger*, problems that one of the most perceptive writers on Wagner has succinctly summed up as 'the streak of cruelty in the humiliation of Hanslich/Beckmesser, which may be there, and a bullying German imperialism in Sachs's final address, which is certainly not.'[1]

Though Wagner's opera conjures up a storybook Nuremberg – picturesque, idyllic, an emblem of the best of old German art and life – no one my age can completely dissociate it from the Nuremberg of the 1930s and 1940s. The Nazis saw to it that we couldn't. Hitler wrote to Wagner's son Siegfried that the sword he was wielding had been forged by Wagner.[2] He commissioned annual performances of *Die Meistersinger* during his Nuremberg rallies,[3] and held the rallies themselves in a stadium built in perverse imitation of the opera's final scene. Nuremberg was also the city that saw the publication of the Führer's detestable anti-Jewish race laws. And of course it was the place where the Nazis went on trial, before an international military tribunal, after their defeat. By that time, Allied bombing had, in less than an hour, obliterated miles of the city's old streets, left the Katherine church a shell, and all but demolished the house of Hans Sachs. What was left of the house was soon pulled down. People said that Nuremberg, the Nazis, Wagner, and *Die Meistersinger* all got what they deserved.[4] And while it is now possible to visit Weimar and pay homage to Goethe without blaming Goethe for the horrors of Buchenwald a few miles away, it is still impossible, for some travellers at least, to visit Nuremberg and not blame Wagner for every horror inflicted by Germans more than a half-century after his death.

Let me speak first to the objections raised against the notorious lines in Hans Sachs's final address. Wagner had had doubts about the address from the start and had decided to strike it from the text when his wife Cosima convinced him, after a full day's discussion, not only to keep the speech but to revise and expand it (with the verses beginning 'Habt Acht!') so that the opera could end with a cautionary statement about the impending Franco-Prussian War.[5] It was, even from an artistic point of view, an ill-advised addition: the new lines can have the effect of reducing the universal aspect of a work that is timeless to the particulars of a nationalistic moment in nineteenth-century history. And it proved to be a disastrous addition when, three generations later, another war, a war with implications for all humanity, loomed over Germany.

In the final address, Sachs cautions Walther, who has refused to accept membership in the master's guild, 'Do not despise the masters, I bid you, but rather honour their art. You owe your happiness today, not to your ancestors, however worthy they may be, nor to your coat of arms, nor to your weapons, your spear and sword, but to the fact that you are a poet, and that a master has accepted you.'

The controversial lines that follow are actually cast in terms of midsummer-mist madness and evil spirits faring abroad on the night before John the Baptist's feast day, but all the same they have been thought sinister, and they constitute a problem that no one writing on *Die Meistersinger* can ignore. Hans Sachs says to Walther, on the penultimate page of the score, 'Take care. Evil spirits threaten us. If the German Empire and its people should one day fall under a false, foreign[6] rule, then no prince will understand his people any more. They will bring foreign mists and foreign vanity to our German land, and no one will know any more what is really German – unless what is really German has continued to live on in our German masters. So I say to you' (and we must remember again that Sachs is singing here to the recalcitrant Walther), 'Honour your German masters. Respect what they did, and you will conjure up *good* spirits. Then, even if the Holy Roman Empire[7] should fade away in the mist, we will still have with us here our Holy German Art.'

The passage was used as propaganda by the Nazis. 'Honour your German masters' was made to mean, not 'Honour the mastersingers of the past'[8] but 'Acknowledge that we Germans are the master race.' It was a gross misreading. Andrew Porter, who is no German, rightly remarks, 'The passage is not bombastic. It is marked *piano*.' He recalls how the German baritone Theo Adam always sang the passage with an almost elegiac dignity, so that it meant what it was supposed to mean – that the good things in German tradition could be lost if the old German masters were no longer revered.[9] The New Grove Encyclopedia entry on Wagner also insists that the passage is not militarist; quite the contrary, it is an affirmation that art is more important for a nation's survival than military might. Thomas Mann wrote that the lines actually 'prove how totally intellectual and apolitical

Wagner's nationalism was.'[10] John Warrack, in the most significant book on *Die Meistersinger* in recent years, sensibly observes that when Wagner wrote the passage, it 'would have seemed to no-one any more objectionable as an expression of love of country and anxiety about foreign threat than John of Gaunt's speech about England in *Richard II*; and it is only in the light of the then-distant future horrors of German nationalism that it has caused distaste.'[11]

The sentiments expressed in Hans Sachs's speech are hardly unique. The stage director Harry Kupfer feels them today, in a Germany threatened by the pervasiveness of what he calls an American 'unculture.'[12] France has entertained a similar love-hate attitude towards all things American, and for much longer. Canadians are constantly told by their media, and even by their government, that their national identity is in imminent danger of being overwhelmed by movies and television from south of the border. British scholars in my academic field, classics, often express a desperate disdain for, and even a fear of, what they regard as the intellectually inferior researches of Americans and Germans alike. The sentiments in these and other nations are not always admirable, but perhaps they are, given the circumstances, understandable.

All the same, the director-driven deconstructionist productions of *Die Meistersinger* so prevalent today persist in misreading Hans Sachs's exhortation; when they deck the *Festwiese* scene with swastikas, they do it unopposed because the slightest opposition is likely to brand an objector as politically incorrect if not an actual Holocaust denier. But we have every reason to object to these weird excesses. Charles Rosen says, apropos of the swastikas and newsreel images that swamp the stage as Hans Sachs bids his Germans respect their artistic heritage, 'When an American lecturer exhorts us to continue reading Emerson, Whitman, and Mark Twain, I do not think we should feel obliged to flash slides of Abu Ghraib and Guantánamo on the screen.'[13] The cultural achievements of a nation's past are themselves a rebuke to the moral failures of its present. There is no need to dishonour the one with the infamy of the other.

The Germany celebrated in the choruses that open and close *Die Meistersinger* is a nation renewing its confidence, not in chauvinistic nationalism, but in the enduring value of art, love, and faith. That Germany has risen again in our lifetimes, and *Die Meistersinger*, with its baptisms and its waving banners, has rightly become again the festival work in Germany's more than seventy opera houses. Today, some three generations after the fall of the Nazis, the opera should be an answer to the neo-Nazism that can still threaten Germany and other countries, for it is ultimately an affirmation of the triumph of beauty and humanity over irrationality and self-destruction.

It is immensely sad that great art can be made to serve evil purposes. Homer's *Iliad* was used by Alexander the Great to justify his bloodiest conquests. Virgil, on his deathbed, wanted his *Aeneid* burned – and I think, with Hermann Broch, who fled the Nazis, that Virgil feared *inter alia* that the *Aeneid*, and in particular the central lines spoken by the hero's father, might be used by imperial Rome as a mandate to subdue and oppress.[14] The Bible itself, though much more than a work of art, has been used to justify evil. So, it need hardly be said, has the Koran. Great works of art and faith can be grossly misinterpreted, and we ought to remind ourselves, if art and faith are any concern to us, that no one interpretation, certainly no reductive interpretation, of them is the only one, or the right one. Wagner has Hans Sachs say, when Beckmesser suggests that one level, a biblical level, might suffice for the true reading of Walther's song, 'You're pretty far off if you think that.' Art means many things, and great art is rich in meanings. It is an abuse of art to limit its interpretation to a single line of thought, let alone a false line of thought. A true work of art radiates meaning on meaning outwards.

The second problem concerns Wagner's treatment of Beckmesser, often cited, even by those who love *Die Meistersinger*, as a major blemish on the work. I cannot agree. Wagner's Beckmesser is likeable even in his spite, and in performance he often steals the show.[15] More importantly, the treatment eventually meted out to him is *required*, on whatever level we read the opera. If the opera is a fairy tale, and in part it is, then the dragon must be slain by the knight in shining armour in order that the maiden in distress be rescued; that is what happens in stories about knights. If the opera is an elaborate baptismal allegory replete with Christian symbols, and in part it is, then the devil must be exorcised; that is what happens at baptisms. If the opera is a comedy true to comic traditions, and it is very much that, then, as in Shakespeare the braggart Falstaff must be plucked and tickled

and the vainglorious Malvolio must be utterly humili-
ated,[16] as in Italian opera the malicious Doctor Bartolo
must be outwitted and the presumptuous Don Pasquale
must be bamboozled, as any number of comic villains
and fools in Aristophanes and Plautus, in Ben Jonson and
Molière, must get their comeuppances, so the foolish
Beckmesser must be outwitted and humbled; that correcting is what comedy is all about, and always has been.
Classic Greek comedy needed to deflate a self-deceived
alazon, and Roman comedy needed to chasten a postur-
ing *miles gloriosus*, in order to restore order to a society
thrown into confusion.

All the same, I like the recent productions of *Die Meistersinger* in which Beckmesser comes on at the end, drag-
ging his lute behind him, to hear the song he has stolen
properly sung. He really listens for once, and he learns
something. This is not in Wagner's stage directions, but it
is justified in his text: Sachs says, after Beckmesser has
stolen the song, 'He won't keep up his malice for long.
Many a man throws away his reason and yet, even with
that, he eventually finds his way home. An hour of weakness comes for everyone – and then he sees how foolish
he is and allows himself to be spoken to.'[17]

Of late, however, Beckmesser's treatment in the opera
has been cast in a decidedly sinister light by a coterie, a ver-
itable cottage industry, of academic writers who shall go
unnamed here. (Anyone interested can find their names
and works cited in the rebuttals made by David Dennis,
Bryan Magee, Charles Rosen, and Hans Rudolf Vaget
listed in my endnotes and bibliography.) We are asked
first to believe, on the basis of a reckless statement made

by Theodor Adorno in *In Search of Wagner* ('All the rejects of Wagner's works are caricatures of Jews'),[18] that Wagner's mature operas not only contain anti-Semitic caricatures but are encoded throughout with anti-Semitic messages. These coded messages have for more than a century escaped the attention of critics and public alike, but now, the coterie tell us, the truth is out at last. They have cracked Wagner's code. Actually, what they have done is to bend every effort to accomplish what the Nazis were unable to do – reduce Wagner's work to the basest level of racial hatred. And, I hope to show, they have failed.

The coterie are certainly right in saying that Wagner was a particularly nasty example of the anti-Semitism that, in his day, was rife all across Europe. But Wagner wrote volume after volume explaining himself and his work, and never once did he indicate even slightly that the operas contained any anti-Semitic coding. Neither did Hitler at any time invoke Wagner's name to justify his anti-Jewish policies.[19] Nor did the rabid Nazi propaganda machine, eager to use Wagner's anti-Semitism for its purposes, ever even insinuate that any of his characters was a Jewish stereotype; there is not a single reference to Beckmesser as Jewish in the whole voluminous output of extant Nazi material.[20]

Still, the coterie insist that (1) an oblique reference to a Grimm folk tale, 'The Jew in the Bramble Bush,' in the second *Stollen* of Walther's Act I trial song (Backmesser is at the time in the marker's booth) is somehow proof that anti-Semitism is woven into the whole ideological fabric of *Die Meistersinger*; that (2) Beckmesser's serenade is a malicious and deliberate parody of Jewish cantorial style; that (3) Beckmesser's limping and twitching in Hans Sachs's workshop is anti-Jewish stereotyping; and that (4) Jewish communities in Vienna and Berlin saw Beckmesser as an anti-Semitic caricature and protested violently. But apart from the one suggestion – if it is a suggestion at all – that Wagner wanted us to associate Beckmesser in the marker's booth with 'the Jew in the Bramble Bush' (an association not noticed by anyone onstage or anyone in the audience until one coterie member made the connection more than a hundred years after the opera premiered),[21] there is not a single anti-Semitic allusion in the entire opera. Nor is there any documented trace of Jewish cantorial style in Beckmesser's serenade; the music is markedly Germanic in its outlines, and Wagner thought enough of it to use it as the *cantus firmus* for the immense finale to Act II that involves every character in the opera. Nor is Beckmesser's limping and twitching in Act III evidence of any perceived 'Jewishness'; they are clearly the result of his having been pummelled by David in the Act II riot. Nor is there any real evidence that the protests made by Jews in German-speaking lands were caused by Beckmesser's serenade or by anything else in *Die Meistersinger*; the hostile reactions by both press and public at performances of the opera were a quite justified response to Wagner's infamous pamphlet 'Judaism in Music,' which he foolishly published for the first time under his own name within a year of the *Meistersinger* premiere.[22]

The plain fact of the matter is that, unlike the Shylock of Shakespeare and the Fagin of Dickens, Sixtus Beck-

messer in *Die Meistersinger* is not depicted as Jewish at all.
He is a typical German pedant with an echt-German
name. Anyone labouring in the groves of academe has
seen him and heard him many times at committee meetings and on faculty councils, picking away at small
points, unimaginative, literal in the extreme, forever
missing the forest for the trees, mirthless but often the
unwitting object of mirth. Yet one industrious coterie
member insists that no production of *Die Meistersinger* is
valid today unless Wagner's contentious town clerk is
depicted as a victimized Jew.[23] The coterie are not dis-
posed to see any significance in the fact that generations
of Jews have loved, listened to, sung in, played in, and
conducted Wagner performances the world over. They
will have it that, though those unfortunates have been
duped into thinking that there is no anti-Semitism in *Die
Meistersinger*, at least *they* haven't.

Two members of the coterie, painfully aware that their
'discoveries' have not found wide acceptance in scholarly
circles, have now qualified their first statements to the
extent of saying that 'Jewishness' is only one of many
potential interpretations one could make about Beckmesser; they have even admitted that the whole opera
cannot be defined exclusively by what they see as its anti-
Semitic context.[24] That has not prevented their grotesque
'dark underside' from making its way into virtually all
handbooks on opera written in the last decade. Repeat a
lie often enough and, for some people, it becomes fact.[25]

Dark underside? Bernard Levin, who is Jewish, and
more aware than most critics that Wagner can be 'dangerous,' cites *Die Meistersinger* as 'the one work of his that

has no darkness in it.' He finds the Act III quintet 'the most light-filled music ever written' and calls the opera 'a benediction on all mankind, if all mankind would simply listen to it.'[26]

CHAPTER FIVE

Wagner and
the Wonder of Art

Given during the first intermission of the first broadcast from the Metropolitan Opera after the destruction of the World Trade Center in New York on September 11, 2001.

We begin this new broadcast season still feeling the loss of, and proudly remembering the selfless courage of, many people in this city and in this country. It may seem inappropriate to be remembering them with a comedy. But *Die Meistersinger* is no ordinary comedy. It can help us, as all great art can. For it ponders the madness that sometimes affects human lives, even as it celebrates the mutual interdependence of our lives and, above all, the importance of art in our civilizations.

One of the wonders of *Die Meistersinger* is that it is a work of art that is about *creating* a work of art – and it does this, not just in a prodigious outpouring of melody but also, in the text, in a pattern of images and metaphors that gather and cluster and grow in meaning, and finally constitute a whole aesthetic.

And that – aesthetics, the study of the nature of art, what it means and why we need it – is what I would like to consider briefly this afternoon as we listen together.

What is art? Why do we produce it? Why do some works of art seem to us of greater significance than others? I am sure that you have, at one time or another, asked yourself such questions. They are hardly new.

Two of our earliest thinkers in the West have said in their different ways that art is fundamentally a *mimesis* – an imitation. The human animal imitates reality, creating because there *is* creation and he is alive with it. Plato taught that art imitates reality at what, today, we might call three degrees of separation. And Aristotle taught that art gives us the universal aspects of reality that otherwise we might know only from particulars.

Wagner knew that. In the act we have just heard, the mastersingers of Nuremberg, who seem to know more about rules and particulars than about nature and life, ask young Walther where he learned the art of singing, and he answers that he learned it in the wintry stillness of his castle, by his fireside, reading an old book of poems by Walther von der Vogelweide – that is to say, Walther of the bird-meadow. And then, Walther says, when spring came and the earth was full of sound, he learned still more from the meadow birds themselves. In short, he learned first not from rules but by *mimesis*. And from that moment on, Wagner gives us a whole pattern of imagery that courses through the music: the songbird becomes a metaphor for the poet.

The foremost thinker of the Middle Ages thought of art primarily in terms of beauty – but defined it simply as the *recta ratio factibilium*, the 'right way of making something.' Poetry is, after all, just a Greek word for making, and for Thomas Aquinas, there would be no fundamental difference between making a good poem and making a good shoe: a proper organization of the parts will *naturally* result in a thing of beauty. In the New Criticism of my undergraduate days, understanding poetry was understanding how the separate elements of poetry – words, sounds, and images – came together to make a poem. Art, according to this aesthetic, is good craftsmanship.

Wagner knew that. Young David, learning his craft from Hans Sachs, tells Walther in the first act, 'Schumacherei und Poeterei, die lern' ich da alleinerlei.' 'Shoemaking and poetry, I'm learning them both at the same time ... how to sole the shoe with a well-fitted stanza.' And from that moment on, through the rest of the opera, the well-made shoe becomes a metaphor for the well-made song.

In modern times, the aesthetic question asked became less 'What is art?' and more 'Are there any objective standards, or is our appreciation of art relative, a matter of personal choice?' Santayana and others have said that, when we contemplate a work of art, we project our own emotions onto it, and it becomes beautiful to us. It is not really a case of 'I know what I like' or 'I like what I know,' but 'You can only see in a work of art what, to some degree, you already have within *yourself*.' Those who do not like, say, Bach have not yet developed in *themselves* a consciousness of, and a feeling for, what Bach is doing in his music.

Hans Sachs knows that. One can always *learn* to like, even love, what one does not at first understand, and he shows this in the opera from beginning to end. He has no patience with the false maxim 'de gustibus.' He knows that taste can be cultivated and horizons can be expanded. And throughout the opera we watch all the people of Nuremberg, including its masters, grow in the knowledge and love of music that is innovative and new to them, music that requires that they go out of themselves to hear the beauty in it.

A deeper question asked in aesthetics is 'How does an

imperfect man find it in him to make beautiful things?'
That is a question often asked about Wagner himself. We
will get Wagner's answer to it, metaphorically as always,
near the start of the act we are about to hear. As Hans
Sachs sits beneath his elder tree making a shoe, he wonders about Walther's song: how could such a young hot-
head possibly have made eight notes of music into a
strain so beautiful that now he can't get it out of his
head?:

Well, Sachs concludes, 'A song bird sings because it is his
nature to sing. There is a sweet compulsion that *drives*
him to sing. And because he *must* sing, he *can*.' Any artist
worthy of the name will tell you of that compulsion: an
artist creates because he has to. And that compulsion not
only *demands* that he exceed his limitations; it *enables* him
to do so.

Then there is the really profound question about art:
'What does it mean?' Wagner's philosopher of choice,
and a major influence on his greatest works, was Arthur
Schopenhauer, who held that art expresses, in words or
in shapes or (most powerfully) in music, an otherwise
imperceptible reality that, for good or – far more often –
for ill, operates in human lives. Schopenhauer called it

Wille. Hans Sachs, in a moment of profound and even pessimistic introspection, calls it *Wahn.*

Perhaps the best translation of that difficult word, for this new century, is 'the irrational.' Unreason, for better or worse, acts in the lives of us apparently reasoning creatures. It runs through each of us like a flaw in bright metal. It can be terribly destructive; it can also be, Wagner says, the potential source of our finest art. But it has to be directed. In the soliloquy 'Wahn, Wahn' in Act III, at the great heart of this opera, Hans Sachs, poring over a book of history, wonders about the endless succession of miseries the race has passed through, ponders the ambivalent force, *Wahn,* that drives us to destruction – and then he rises from his book, goes to his window, sees morning light break over the rooftops of his city, and vows to direct that irrational, potentially destructive force, *Wahn,* to good ends. When Walther comes to him with a song that has welled up in him in a dream (that most irrational of human experiences), Sachs tells him that the truest revelation of *Wahn* comes to us in dreams. He helps Walther fashion his midsummer night's dream into a work of art – and into no ordinary work of art, but into a song that solves the problems that, the night before, had beset his beloved city.

And as always in this opera, there is a metaphor that supports this. Baptism. Art can have an almost sacramental power, a power to cleanse, to *save* us from our *Wahn.* (Schopenhauer himself had suggested a correlation between his concept of *Wille* and the Christian doctrine of original sin, from which baptism redeems the believer.) All of *Die Meistersinger* takes place on the eve and the feast of John the Baptist. Hans Sachs is named for John the Baptist. At the opera's start, the people of Nuremberg hymn their hope that the Baptist will lift them up by the river Jordan. And the song that Sachs helps Walther create out of his *Wahn*, the song he christens, the song he slyly arranges to be sung at the river Pegnitz in the last scene – that song brings a great wash of cleansing and rebirth (Wagner's own word is redemption) to all the characters whose lives have been thrown awry by the madness of *Wahn*.

And so to our last question – 'Why do we need art?' I don't suppose that Leontyne Price ever considered herself a philosopher, but she answered that question once, before a senate panel, pleading for national support of the arts and citing Herodotus, who spoke some twenty-five centuries ago of an ancient people who succeeded in conquering other nations – but are now buried in obscurity because they produced no artists. Art is the expression of a people, and it still speaks when empires pass away. So, in his last great solo at the opera's end, Hans Sachs tells Walther, the young knight with a sword and a song, that the survival of his civilization, of his Germany, depends not on making war but on creating and preserving great works of art. And that, he says, is something the masters of Nuremberg, whatever their faults, have always known. Walther must respect that.

Deepest of all, however, we need art if we are to deal with the inevitable sadness in our lives. Wagner only allows Hans Sachs one line about the great loss he suffered in the past. 'Hatt' einst ein Weib und Kinder genug,' he tells Eva. 'I once had a wife and children enough to satisfy me.' The historical Hans Sachs lost his wife and seven children, probably from the plague. Wagner's Hans Sachs has nurtured a hope of marrying Eva and having children again. But, in the act we are about to hear, he realizes that he must resign himself and give her up to the younger poet with whom she has fallen in love. *It is Sachs's dedication to his art that enables him to make that sacrifice.* Wagner tells us this, not in words, but in the prelude to Act III, where themes associated with selfless renunciation, humble shoe-making, and ennobling art come together, and we look into the soul of Hans Sachs. Here is the 'Renunciation Theme' that begins Act III and will recur, with almost tragic poignancy, in all of its great moments:

Can we sum up Wagner's aesthetic, as expressed in *Die Meistersinger*, in the half-minute that remains to us before we listen to the rest of his opera? If we read the music and the metaphors rightly, we can say five things. Art, for Richard Wagner, is fashioned from both intuition and honest craftsmanship, from both innovating spirit and respect for tradition. It can speak powerfully to us if we have within ourselves the capacity to respond to it. It can survive the fall of empires to speak to future civilizations about the civilization that produced it. It can tell us what we need to know about ourselves, perhaps most of all about the flaw in human nature that makes mysteries of our lives. And it can help us to accept the inevitable sadness in life – as well as to sing like songbirds from the sheer joy of being alive.

CHAPTER SIX

Recordings and DVDs

Given the length and complexity of *Die Meistersinger*, it should come as no surprise that, though some of the recordings made of it are very fine indeed, no one of them does the work complete justice. (There is some music, as Artur Schnabel has reminded us, that is greater than it can be performed.) Out of the thirty-odd recordings that pass in and out of availability, I have selected ten that I have found, for various reasons, outstanding. At the time of printing, all of them are available on the labels indicated, though some may have to be specially ordered, and the lesser-known labels may not provide libretti. My listings follow chronologically, except that I shall save for last the performance I regard as best of all.

Mono

The 1936 live broadcast under Artur Bodanzky from the Metropolitan Opera has sound that is poor even for its day, and is disfigured by the cuts that were standard then outside of Germany. It is nonetheless vibrant and vivid, graced with the Eva of the beloved Elisabeth Rethberg and dominated by perhaps the greatest of all Hans Sachses, Friedrich Schorr. (From Music and Arts)

The 1937 live performance from the Salzburg Festival, conducted by Arturo Toscanini, is complete to the last note – and is in fact the only complete recording of a Wagner opera we have from the Maestro. Long available on various pirate labels in desperately poor sound, it has now been almost miraculously restored by Ward Marston and Seth Winter – though the woodwinds can still sound more up front than the mighty choruses. The cast, headed by Hans Hermann Nissen and Maria Reining, is a strong one, and the performance – it is no surprise to discover – sings out as no other recorded performance does. (From Andante)

The 1943 live recording from the Bayreuth Festival has magisterial, insightful conducting by Wilhelm Furtwängler, but generally poor singing – and two large sections of the performance, including the quintet, are missing. (From Music and Arts and Opera d'Oro) Another recording from the 1943 festival, conducted by Furtwängler's alternate, Hermann Abendroth, is complete – as are all the recommended recordings to follow – and, with its generally good singing and remarkably good sound, actually gives a better idea than the Furtwängler does of what Bayreuth performances were like in that desperate year when it was imperative that German audiences be told that art was saner and more lasting than military might. (From Preiser)

The 1950 recording under Hans Knappertsbusch was the first *Meistersinger* made in the studio and is by critical consensus the best mono version. The tempi, on the slow side, nonetheless seem unfailingly right while the music is unfolding, and an atmosphere of *Gemütlichkeit* pervades every scene. There are outstanding contributions from Paul Schöffler (Hans Sachs), Hilde Gueden (Eva), and Anton Dermota (David), and a classic, if cartoonish, Beckmesser from Karl Dönch. The sound, however, is no better than good, and the Walther is something of a liability. (From Decca) The genial Kna' can also be heard conducting a 1952 live performance from Bayreuth, but again he has tenor trouble. (From Melodram)

The 1951 live recording from Bayreuth under Herbert von Karajan, a best-seller in its day, has the feeling of an actual performance at Wagner's theatre and features a charming Eva from Elisabeth Schwarzkopf. But the rest of the singing is variable, and orchestral details are not always clear. (From Myto and Urania)

The 1956 studio recording from Berlin was thought for many years to be the classic set. Rudolf Kempe's conducting has a wonderful warmth and resonance, Elisabeth Grümmer is quite the best Eva on records, and Benno Kusche is pretty close to being the best Beckmesser. But Rudolph Schock, a veteran of operetta, is miscast as Walther, and all the voices tend to blanket the orchestra. It was time to move on to stereo. (From EMI)

Stereo

The 1963 live recording conducted by Joseph Keilberth preserves the performance that reopened the Nationaltheater in Munich the day after (and in Europe closer to the very day of) the assassination of President John F. Kennedy. Intended to mark the postwar emergence of a Germany newly dedicated to the arts of peace, with two Americans, Jess Thomas and Claire Watson, as Walther and Eva, it has a palpable feeling of both triumph and tragedy about it. Many critics are so put off by the virtually unlistenable Hans Sachs that they undervalue the whole performance; others have an special affection for the recording, and its stature has grown with the years. (From BMG)

The 1976 studio recording from Berlin, conducted by Eugen Jochum with sure pacing and unfailingly beautiful detail, has to make do with an Eva who, despite what Sachs tells her in Act III, thinks she is singing Isolde. It also has a Walther who couldn't conceivably have come 'aus Frankenland' and a Hans Sachs who clearly never cobbled a shoe in all his life. All the same, a century hence this set will be a collector's item – not for its Eva, but for its Walther and Hans Sachs. There it has two of the greatest singers of the twentieth century, Plácido Domingo and Dietrich Fischer-Dieskau. Walther and Sachs aren't exactly roles those gentlemen were born to sing, but by sheer intelligence and musicianship, they make indelible impressions in them. Didn't Sachs say in Act II that a songbird sings because he must and, because he must, he finds in his heart the power to sing what he otherwise could not? Domingo and Fischer-Dieskau are, each of them, that kind of songbird. (From Deutsche-Grammophon)

The 1994 studio recording from Munich (where the Bayerische Staatsoper prides itself in giving annual festival performances of Die Meistersinger without benefit of rehearsal) zips along merrily and, thanks largely to Ben Heppner, a Walther with the right style and heft, was received with rapture when it came out. But it has not worn well: Bernd Weikl's estimable Hans Sachs had, by 1994, grown unsteady, and Wolfgang Sawallisch's conducting lacks that final degree of geniality and generosity that can make the opera a great experience. (From EMI)

The 1995 studio recording from Chicago, a Grammy Award–winner led by Georg Solti (who had led a relatively unsuccessful recording thirty years previous) is magnificent in sound and cast from strength – with Heppner even better than he was with Sawallisch, and with René Pape and Karita Mattila a fine father-daughter team. But José Van Dam (Hans Sachs), past his prime, all but ignores the humour in his role, and there is little sense of drama about the carefully planned proceedings. (From Decca/London)

The best recording, to my mind, was – astonishingly – made in 1967 but not issued worldwide until 1993. (Deutsche-Grammophon, with an eye on the market, withdrew it in favour of the Domingo/Fischer-Dieskau recording.) Here, for the first time, everything is right. The underrated Rafael Kubelick leads the Bavarian Symphony Orchestra in a spacious, beautifully paced, lovingly detailed performance that carefully balances the joyous and the meditative. The stereo sound is remarkably vivid for 1967 (the performance derives from a series of live radio broadcasts). And *mirabile dictu* the cast, which includes Thomas Stewart, Sandor Konya, and Gundula Janowitz, is strong from top to bottom. Highly recommended. (From Arts Music; formerly from Calig and Myto)

Videos and DVDs

There are at present six performances of *Die Meistersinger* available on video and/or DVD. Again, the listing here is chronological, except for the performance I regard as best, which I shall save for last.

The 1970 production from Hamburg, one of thirteen opera films studio-made under the direction of Rolf Liebermann, is fondly remembered from screenings at Wagner Societies the world over, and in 2007 it finally appeared on DVD. It is traditionally set, well-routined, and nicely filmed with a horizontally moving camera that glides knowingly across the sound stages and provides often eloquent close-ups. But the performance suffers from cuts in all three acts: much of David's instruction, a verse each of Sachs's cobbling song and Beckmesser's serenade, the second version of Walther's song, and the dance of the apprentices are all missing. Three Americans take the leads: Richard Cassilly looking terribly uncomfortable as Walther but singing well, Arlene Saunders a delight as Eva, and Giorgio Tozzi an almost Italianate Sachs, his hands as wonderfully expressive as his voice. Leopold Ludwig conducts, rather deliberately at times. Monophonic sound only. Generally good subtitles. (From Arthaus)

The 1988 production from the Sydney Opera House is essential viewing for the Hans Sachs of Donald McIntyre; the veteran baritone may not command the role vocally as he once did, but he gives a multifaceted dramatic reading clearly based on a close study of the text. Otherwise, the performance can boast some charming scenes, most notably that between Sachs and Eva (Helena Döse) in Act II. The camera alertly catches several bits of stage business that neatly characterize Beckmesser, Pogner, and Magdalene. But the overall sound serves Charles Mackerras's conducting poorly, much of the singing is strained, and the production, functional at best, is overly drab until the final *Festwiese*. The subtitles are nicely colloquial but too concise; many subtleties in the text are lost. (From Kultur)

The 1995 production from the Deutsche Oper Berlin is set to no great effect in a dullish, quasi-nineteenth-century Nuremberg. But it has solid conducting by Rafael Frühbeck de Burgos, lively stage direction by Götz Friedrich, good singing and acting from a Hans Sachs (Wolfgang Brendel) who looks younger than Walther (Gösta Winbergh), a plumpish Eva (Eva Johansson), an unthreatening Beckmesser (Eike Wilm Schulte), and a charmingly energetic David (Uwe Peper). It also has free-wheeling but unusually helpful subtitles – a not unimportant matter considering the complexity of the opera's text. What most viewers remember from this production is how Friedrich darkens the stage for Sachs's 'Habt Acht.' (From Arthaus)

The 2001 Metropolitan Opera performance, in a traditional staging by Otto Schenk and Günther Schneider-Siemmsen (characteristically lavish but not so attractive as the previous Met production by Nathaniel Merrill and

Robert O'Hearn), is slowly but solidly paced by James Levine leading the wonderful Met orchestra. There is a lovingly detailed and even touching performance by Thomas Allen as Beckmesser that is required viewing for the 'Beckmesser in the Brambles' bunch. But James Morris, the most famous Wotan of his day, struggles with the role of Hans Sachs and, while Karita Mattila and Ben Heppner give fine vocal performances, they are not as easy to watch in close-up as they were from a distance in the vasty Met. René Pape, unable to disguise his youth, is nonetheless luxury casting as old Pogner. The Met titles will be familiar to anyone who has seen the production in the house. (From Deutsche-Grammophon)

The 2005 production from Zurich is problematic. During the overture we see conductor and cast making merry over a meal, presumably discussing the performance they are about to give – a performance in which, as it turns out, they appear to be having a better time than we are. The new-broom production is intent on sweeping away any remnant of perceived *Meistersinger* Kitsch: there are no churches, no slope-roofed houses, no prancing ingenues playing apprentices, no street brawls, no sunlight streaming through windows, no waving banners for the finale. Just three expensive-looking, severely stylized acts in, respectively, black, blue, and orange hues. In the yawning empty spaces, Peter Seiffert is a hammy but enjoyable Walther and Michael Volle a brawny, extroverted Beckmesser (a good idea that doesn't quite work). José Van Dam's cold, world-weary Sachs will disappoint his many fans. The crisp conducting of Franz Welser-Möst does not always allow the music its natural flow. The subtitling is generally good. (From EMI)

My first choice, then, is a 1984 performance from Bayreuth – a rather modest, low-keyed, amiable production that I saw in the Festspielhaus several times in the 1980s. There is not much scenery to look at, the conducting by Horst Stein is rather slow-paced, and there is perhaps too much subtitling for comfort. But the good things about the performance are very good indeed – the burly Hans Sachs of Bernd Weikl and the endearing Beckmesser of Hermann Prey. (Note that in none of these DVD performances does Beckmesser come across even remotely as the anti-Semitic caricature he is said by some to be.) Weikl looks as if he is dreaming his way through the role of Hans Sachs, and why not? It's every German baritone's dream to sing the part. As a gesture to Germany's conciliatory post-war attitudes, Wolfgang Wagner, the composer's grandson and the producer/director of this production, makes an appearance at the final moment and reconciles Beckmesser and Sachs – who places the laurel wreath Walther has won on a banner adorned with a likeness of King David. Small personal note: a production assistant at Bayreuth once sent me the page on which Weikl took down the Prize Song, still folded over square as it was when Prey pocketed it on stage. (From Deutsche-Grammophon; original video release from Philips)

APPENDIX

TEXTS AND TRANSLATIONS
OF THE SONGS

Hans Sachs's Cobbler's Song

Als Eva aus dem Paradies
  von Gott dem Herrn verstossen,
gar schuf ihr Schmerz der harte Kies
  an ihrem Fuss, dem blossen.
  Das jammerte den Herrn,
  ihr Füsschen hatt' er gern:
und seinem Engel rief er zu:
'Da mach' der armen Sünd'rin Schuh'!
und da der Adam, wie ich seh',
an Steinen dort sich stösst die Zeh',
    das recht fortan
    er wandeln kann,
  so miss' dem auch Stiefeln an!'

O Eva! Eva! Schlimmes Weib,
  das hast du am Gewissen,
das ob der Füss am Menschenleib
  jetzt Engel schustern müssen.
  Bleibst du im Paradies,
  da gab es keinen Kies.
Um deiner jungen Missetat
hantier' ich jetzt mit Ahl' und Draht,
und ob Herrn Adams übler Schwäch'
versohl' ich Schuh' und streiche Pech.
    Wär' ich nicht fein
    ein Engel rein,
  Teufel möchte Schuster sein!

O Eva! Hör mein' Klageruf,
  mein' Not und schwer Verdrüssen!
Die Kunstwerk', die ein Schuster schuf,
  die tritt die Welt mit Füssen!
   Gäb' nicht ein Engel Trost,
     der gleiches Werk erlost,
und rief mich oft ins Paradies,
wie ich da Schuh' und Stiefel liess!
Doch wenn mich der in Himmel hält,
dan liegt zu Fussen mir die Welt,
     Und bin in Ruh'
       Hans Sachs ein Schuh-
   macher und Poet dazu.

When the Lord God turned Eve out of Paradise,
  the stony pebbles hurt her bare feet.
That made the Lord sad.
He liked her little footsies.
And so He called out to his angel,
'Make shoes for this poor sinner!
And since Adam, I see, has banged his toes on the stones,
  measure him for boots so that, in the future,
  he'll be able to walk safely!'

O Eve, Eve, you naughty girl,
  you've got this on your conscience:
Because there are feet on the human body,
  angels have to make shoes now.
If only you'd stayed in Paradise where there were no
  pebbles!
As it is, thanks to your youthful misdeed, I have to
  work with awl and thread.
And because of Mister Adam's disastrous weakness, I have to
  sole shoes and rub on pitch.
Were I not a right good angel,
  the devil might be doing this cobbling!

O Eve, hear my cry of pain,
  My need, the burden of my discontent!
The works of art that the cobbler makes
  the world treads under foot.
If an angel appointed to do work like mine
    did not often console me and summon me to Paradise,
  I would gladly forsake these shoes and boots.
But when he does take me to heaven,
  the world lies at my feet, and I have rest –
  I, Hans Sachs, a shoemaker and a poet too.

Walter's Prize Song: The First Drafts

1. Sung when Sachs invites him to remember his dream

Morgenlich leuchtend in rosigem Schein,
  von Blüt und Duft
  geschwellt die Luft,
  voll aller Wonnen
  nie ersonnen
ein Garten lud mich ein
  Gast ihm zu sein.

Wonnig entragend dem seligen Raum
    bot gold'ner Frucht
    heilsaft'ge Wucht
    mit holdem Prangen
    dem Verlangen
an duft'ger Zweige Saum
    herrlich ein Baum.

    Sei euch vertraut
  welch hehres Wunder mir gescheh'n:
an meiner Seite stand ein Weib,

so hold und schön ich nie geseh'n;
    gleich einer Braut
  umfasste sie sanft meinen Leib;
    mit Augen winkend
    die Hand wies blinkend,
  was ich verlangend begehrt,
  die Frucht so hold und wert
    vom Lebensbaum.

It was like a morning radiant with rosy light.
The scent of flowers filled the air.
A garden of unimaginable happiness
    invited me to be its guest.

And splendidly rising above that blessed enclosure,
offering me its golden, healing fruit,
responding to my desire with the burden of its branches,
    there was a glorious tree.

Let me confide what a miracle befell me then.
At my side there stood a woman,
more beautiful than any I had ever seen before.
She embraced me tenderly, as if she were my bride,
and her eyes were shining as she lifted her hand
to what I ardently desired – the lustrous fruit
    of the Tree of Life.

2. Sung when Sachs asks for more verses

Abendlich glühend in himmlischer Pracht
    verschied der Tag,
    wie dort ich lag;
    aus ihren Augen
    Wonne saugen,
  Verlangen einz'ger Macht
    in mir nur wacht'.

Nächtlich umdämmert der Blick mir sich bricht:
   wie weit so nah'
   beschienen da
   zwei lichte Sterne
   aus der Ferne
durch schlanker Zweige Licht
hehr mein Gesicht.

   Lieblich ein Quell
auf stiller Höhe dort mir rauscht:
jetzt schwellt er an sein hold Getön'
so stark und süss ich's nie erlauscht,
   leuchtend und hell
wie strahlten die Sterne da schön;
   zu Tanz und Reigen
   in Laub und Zweigen
   der gold'nen sammelm sich mehr,
   statt Frucht ein Sternenheer
   im Lorbeerbaum.

It was like an evening when the heavens were aglow
with the departure of day. I lay in the garden taking in
the wonder of her eyes. And a powerful yearning
   rose within me.

It was like night, and my vision grew faint when,
so near and yet so far away, two bright stars appeared.
They shone through the lattice-branches of the tree
   onto my face.

Lovingly, a spring on a silent height murmured to me,
and then its beautiful singing swelled.
I had never heard such a wonderful sound.
The two stars were gleaming, dancing, circling,
entwining amid the tree's leaves and branches.
And the fruit was no longer there. I saw a host of stars
   in the Laurel Tree.

3. Sung when Walther sees Eva in her wedding gown

Weilten die Sterne im lieblichen Tanz?
      So licht und klar
      im Lockenhaar,
      vor allen Frauen
      hehr zu schauen
    lag ihr mit zartem Glanz
      ein Sternenkranz.

Wunder ob Wunder nun bieten sich dar:
      zwiefachen Tag
      ich grüssen mag;
      denn gleich zwei'n Sonnen
      reinster Wonnen,
    der hehrsten Augen Paar
      nahm ich da wahr.

      Huldreichstes Bild,
dem ich zu nahen mich erkühnt;
den Kranz, von zweier Sonnen Strahl
zugleich verblichen und ergrünt,
      minnig und mild,
    sie flocht ihn um das Haupt dem Gemahl.
      Dort Huld-geboren
      nun Ruhm-erkoren,
    giesst paradiesische Lust
    sie in des Dichters Brust
      im Liebestraum.

Did the stars linger in their lovely dance?
Light and clear upon her hair
(honoured above all women to behold)
there lay, delicate and radiant,
    a garland of stars.

Wonder on wonder appeared then.
Daylight seemed to dawn on me twofold:
I looked into her eyes. They were like
two suns of purest rapture.

I made bold to approach that vision full of grace,
and she took the garland made of the beams
of those two suns, dimly seen yet dewy fresh,
and lovingly, gently placed it on her husband's head.
Born in grace, chosen to be honoured, she filled
this poet's heart with the happiness of heaven.
    That was my dream of love.

4. The final version, compressing the three early drafts into one

Morgenlich leuchtend in rosigen Schein,
    von Blüt und Duft
    geschwellt die Luft,
    voll aller Wonnen
    nie ersonnen
    ein Garten lud mich ein –
Dort unter einem Wunderbaum,
    von Früchten reich behangen,
zu schau'n im sel'gen Liebestraum,
    was höchstem Lustverlangen
    Erfüllung kühn verhiess –
        das schönste Weib,
    Eva im Paradies.

Abendlich dämmernd umschloss mich die Nacht;
    auf steilem Pfad
    war ich genaht
    zu einer Quelle
    reiner Welle
    die lockend mir gelacht.
Dort unter einem Lorbeerbaum

von Sternen hell durchschienen,
ich schaut' im wachen Dichtertraum
* von heilig holden Mienen,*
* mich netzend mit dem edlen Nass –*
*   das hehrste Weib,*
* die Muse des Parnass.*

* Huldreichster Tag,*
dem ich aus Dichters Traum erwacht!
Das ich erträumt, das Paradies,
in himmlisch neu verklärter Pracht
* hell vor mir lag,*
dahin lachend nun der Quell den Pfad mir wies;
*   die, dort geboren,*
*   mein Herz erkoren,*
* der Erde lieblichstes Bild,*
* als Muse mir geweiht,*
* so heilig ernst as mild,*
* ward kühn von mir gefreit;*
* am lichten Tag der Sonnen*
* durch Sanges Sieg gewonnen*
* Parnass und Paradies!*

It was like a morning radiant with rosy light.
The scent of flowers filled the air.
A garden of unimaginable happiness
invited me to be its guest.
And there, beneath a wondrous tree
richly laden with fruit,
I was invited to see, in a blessed dream of love,
the fulfilment of my utmost longing –
that most beautiful of women,
Eve in Paradise.

It was like an evening. Twilight enfolded me.
On a steep path I drew near to a spring of pure water.

It laughed and drew me onwards.
And there, beneath a laurel tree,
with stars shining brightly through its branches,
in a poet's waking dream I beheld her.
Her face was gracious and saintly,
and she washed me with water from the sacred spring –
that most wonderful of women,
the Muse of Parnassus.

How blessed was the day
when I awoke from my poet's dream!
The Paradise that I had dreamed of
lay before me in bright, newly transfigured splendour.
The laughing spring now showed me the way to it.
And she who was born there,
the chosen one of my heart,
the loveliest vision on earth,
destined to be my Muse,
as numinous as she is mild,
was eagerly wooed by me.
In the sun's bright daylight
I won, through my supremacy in song,
Parnassus and Paradise!

NOTES

CHAPTER ONE The First *Stollen*

1 Georg Gottfried Gervinus, *Geschichte der poetischen National-Litera-tur der Deutschen* (1835–42). This history and a later handbook by Gervinus provided Wagner with two of the most memorable features of Act III of his opera: a description of the historical Hans Sachs grown melancholic in his old age, given to reading silently, answering only with a nod of the head; and details of the master-singers' practice of 'baptizing' a new song in the presence of 'god-fathers.' See Warrack 1994, 3.

2 Actually the 1845 sketch, which shows clear signs of hasty composition, runs to some 1200 words. It is a virtually complete synopsis of the opera to come twenty years later, but some of the differences are interesting. Act I takes place in the Nuremberg church of St Sebaldus (a more important church historically and architecturally than St Katherine's, but not the place where the masters met). Walther, Eva, and Beckmesser are called only 'the young man,' 'the girl,' and 'the Marker.' (By 1861 they were named, respectively, Konrad, Emma, and Hanslich. Only David and Magdalene have their names as early as 1845, which seems to indicate that the biblical pattern I trace in this book was developed by Wagner over several years.) 'The young man' chooses Siegfried and Parzifal as the subjects of his trial song. 'The Marker' is more waspish in the sketch than Beckmesser is in the completed opera, and Sachs is more cynical – malicious and mistrusted by the others. The opera's warm humanity and its Schopenhauerian dimension still lay in the future.

3 The first clear indication that Wagner thought of his *Meistersinger* as the equivalent of an Athenian satyr play came in *Eine Mitteilung*

an Meine Freunde (*A Communication to My Friends*) in 1851; Sachs
had by then become a genial character, and he and 'the Marker'
had taken over centre stage. By 1861, with a second prose draft,
Wagner, doubtless under the influence of Schopenhauer, had come
to identify less with Walther and more with Sachs. (A similar
development had occurred during the evolution of the *Ring* text,
as Wagner's interest shifted from Siegfried to Wotan.)

4 The incident, the truth of which there is no reason to doubt, is
recorded in *Mein Leben* (*My Life*, 107): in a Nuremberg tavern in
1835 Wagner's brother-in-law passed him off as the famous singer
Luigi Lablache, and the riot resulted when a local carpenter gave
in Wagner's presence an unintentionally hilarious demonstration
of bad singing. When the noisiest of the brawlers hit the ground
with a thump, Wagner recalled that 'as if by magic the whole
crowd dispersed in every direction ... I was able to stroll arm-in-
arm with my brother-in-law through the lonely moonlit streets.'

5 Much of Wagner's loving picture of old Nuremberg and several
details in his plot – including the song competition – come from
Hoffmann's stories 'Norika' and 'Master Martin the Cooper and
His Apprentices,' which Bizet, some time before he wrote *Carmen*,
thought of setting to music.

6 Wagner's Nuremberg is a Romantic construct. His opera says
nothing about the sixteenth-century city's importance in international trade, of its banking houses, of its religious diversity, or of its
political and class conflicts. By Wagner's day Nuremberg was a
still picturesque but fossilized city, first sent into decline by the
shifting trade routes and the Thirty Years' War and thereafter suffering from changes effected by the Napoleonic Wars, the Indus-
trial Revolution, and the unstoppable movement towards German
unification under Prussia. At the same time, Nuremberg had
become a nostalgic symbol of a German past in which stability,
industriousness, and dedication to the arts prevailed – a concept
taken up enthusiastically by right-leaning nationalists in the twentieth century. Some critics have seen Wagner's idealization of
Nuremberg's past as setting a dangerous precedent: the city came
to have an almost cultic significance, which the Nazis exploited.

For a perceptive discussion of this, with special reference to Wieland Wagner's postwar production of *Die Meistersinger* at Bayreuth (which deliberately eliminated every trace of old Nuremberg), see McFarland 1983. For a much fuller discussion of the city (a discussion that, alas, remains rather obtuse about the opera), see Brockmann 2006. The matter of Nuremberg's mythic significance for Romantic Germans is also touched on, along with several other issues, in an imaginary – and very witty – exchange between Wagner and a professorial Internet browser in Höyng 2002; the pertinent pages are 130–2.

7   The first of the 'vier gekrönte Töne' in Wagenseil's *De Sacri Rom. Imperii libera civitate Norinbergensi commentatio* suggested both the opening 'Mastersingers' theme of the overture and the 'Banner' theme that follows it. See Warrack, 64 and 121–2. Puschmann's volume was titled *Gründlicher Bericht des deutschen Meistergesangs*; Grimm's was titled *Ueber den altdeutschen Meistergesang*.

8   'Hans Sachsens poetische Sendung' ('Hans Sachs's Poetical Mission'), a early poem of Goethe's that seems to have begun the tradition, widely accepted in Wagner's day, of Nuremberg as a symbol of a peaceful, hard-working community where German art and craftsmanship flourished as nowhere else.

9   The 1840 Lortzing piece is based on an 1827 play by Johann Ludwig Deinhardstein that Wagner had certainly seen. Its plot differs in amusing ways from Wagner's: Sachs actually enters the singing contest in Nuremberg in order to win the hand of Kunegunde, the daughter of a wealthy jeweller; he is defeated by a foppish member of the town council, leaves Nuremberg, but is reinstated by an admirer of his poetry who turns out to be the Emperor Maximilian. So in the end Sachs gets the girl.

10   There were other singing schools, some of them flourishing as early as 1400, in Mainz, Augsburg, Freiburg, Strassburg, and elsewhere. Nuremberg took the lead in the sixteenth century, thanks to the leadership of Hans Sachs, who authored more than four thousand mastersongs as well as several volumes of poems and dramas. The mastersingers themselves were never so popular or respected as Wagner represents them, but they did preserve a

respect for art, morality, and religious values through two turbulent centuries.

11 Some plot synopses mistakenly describe Act I as taking place in the morning, as the opening hymn is followed by a *Singschule*, the public recital that generally followed a morning service. But David emphatically says that the masters are meeting for a *Freiung* (an audition), not a *Singschule*, and the masters generally held the *Freiung* between midday and evening song.

12 Perry Como, an American crooner of the forties and fifties, once had the Vienna Choir Boys on his television show and asked a young David among his guests what he had to do to join the ranks. He was told emphatically, 'You haff gott to be a goot zinger!'

13 To spare my listeners too many technical terms I used 'song' in my lecture for what the old mastersingers (and Wagner as well, but with some inconsistency) called a *Bar*: an AAB set of *Stollen, Stollen*, and *Abgesang*. I have kept 'song' in preference to 'Bar' in this book.

14 The more likely meaning of *Stollen* in mastersinger terminology is 'support': the two *Stollen* are the two symmetrical columns on which the *Abgesang*, like the entablature of a Greek temple, is placed. The troubadours had called the corresponding segments of their songs *pedes* (supports).

15 The rules for mastersinging excluded romantic love as a subject and favoured biblical, moral, and didactic themes. The mastersinger guilds, almost exclusively male in composition, took for their insignia the image of King David and his harp, an emblem of spiritual rather than secular song. So Walther all but precipitates his own failure by opting, in his trial song, for personal emotion and images from nature – the province of the medieval minnesingers and especially of his namesake Walther von der Vogelweide. The minnesingers (singers of love) had also had their contests, one of which Wagner put on the stage in Act II of *Tannhäuser*, where the subject chosen is love and where Walther von der Vogelweide is one of the contestants.

16 It should be noted that when Wagner sketched the first prose draft of *Die Meistersinger* he had never heard of Hanslick, who was only

twenty years old in 1845 and had yet to publish a single review; that Hanslick's first published article was an extensive and very favourable review of *Tannhäuser*, for which Wagner wrote a long letter of thanks; that the name Veit Hanslich appeared only in Wagner's second prose draft, and stayed there for little more than two months. Hanslick's reviews had turned critical when, after *Lohengrin*, he came to see Wagner as an enemy of classicism in music. He nonetheless accepted an invitation from a friend to hear Wagner's reading of the *Meistersinger* text at a soirée in Vienna in 1862. In his autobiography he records that he found the text 'an appealing, sometimes merry and sometimes moving picture of life and customs of German town life.' He makes no mention of the character of Beckmesser at all. It was Wagner who wrote, in *Mein Leben* (*My Life*, 704), that Hanslick saw the opera as directed against him, turned pale and angry, and left at the end of the reading. Whoever is right about what happened that night, Hanslick's review of the Munich premiere was favourable, but not altogether so: the overture was 'positively brutal in its effect,' Hans Sachs sounded like 'an infuriated hyena' in his cobbling song, the Leitmotif system was 'erroneous in principle and unlovely and unmusical in its steadfast implementation,' and the opera itself was 'a pathological symptom.' Later in life he regretted writing the review in haste and resentment over the opera's success, and 'came to prefer *Die Meistersinger* to all other Wagner operas with the possible exception of *Tannhäuser*' (Pleasants 1950, 29).

CHAPTER TWO   The Second *Stollen*

1 The scent of the elder, an aphrodisiac, and of the linden, which in folklore induced enchanted sleep, are particularly appropriate for an act that is famous for the spell it casts. Nuremberg took as its symbol an ancient linden tree that grew in its confines. The linden was also immortalized by Walther von der Vogelweide in his poem 'Unter der Linden.' It has been objected that 'Flieder' properly means 'lilac,' and that the lilac did not exist in Germany in Hans Sachs's day (and in any case would certainly not be blossoming in

midsummer). But 'Flieder' is also used for the elder tree, and the elder is a perennial that, in medieval Germany, was thought to ward off evil spirits.

2 In the fifteenth century Nuremberg's cityscape caused the learned humanist Aeneas Silvius Piccolomini (later Pope Pius II) to exclaim: 'What a splendid appearance this city presents! How clean the streets, how elegant the houses!' In the eighteenth century Mozart, reflecting the tastes of his day, wrote to his sister, 'We had breakfast in Nuremberg – an ugly city.' In the nineteenth century Nuremberg's medieval picturesqueness again caught the fancy of Romantics like Heinrich Wachenroder and Ludwig Tieck.

3 My wise and witty copy-editor, John St James, is reminded at this point of a lyric by Oscar Hammerstein II: 'And somewhere a bird who is bound he'll be heard is throwing his heart at the sky.'

4 The historical Sachs lived from 1494 to 1576, and was twice married. Kunegunde Kreuzer bore him seven children, all of whom predeceased him, along with their mother, possibly of plague. His second wife, Barbara Harscher, had six children from an earlier marriage. The action of Wagner's opera may be thought then to take place in midsummer of 1560 or 1561, the only summers when Sachs was a childless widower. He would have been in his early sixties. The playful tenderness in Wagner's music for the scene between Sachs and Eva may owe something to the fact that he did not himself become a father until he was fifty-one years of age and resuming work on *Die Meistersinger*, and that 'the last twenty years of his life were spent in the company of young children ... Cosima's diaries make it clear that he was a devoted father with a playful streak in his nature' (Matthews 1983, 9–10).

5 Recorded in Spencer 2000, 180.

6 *Cosima Wagner's Diaries* 1978, entry for 8 December 1872.

CHAPTER THREE   The *Abgesang*

1 Gervinus's history (see note 1 in chapter 1) described Sachs thus, and Goethe's early poem (see note 8 in chapter 1) presented him

'reflecting on life and art while relaxing in his workshop on a Sunday morning' (McFarland 1983, 28).

2 David has to make three vigorous efforts to draw the attention of his master away from his book. This is a charming instance of what might be called the 'running slave' routine from old Roman comedy: the servant comes back from an errand, mission accomplished, and the master does not, or pretends he does not, notice him despite his repeated calls for attention. Magdalene, similarly, makes three trips back to her pew to fetch things for a distracted Eva in Act II. (In Act I of Mozart's *Don Giovanni* Leporello runs in, mission accomplished, and draws three cries of 'bravo!' from his master, who, to demonstrate his superior awareness of the developing situation, elicits in turn three cries of 'bravo!' from his servant. The routine is wittily capped by a 'bravo, bravo, archibravo!' from the master.)

3 The passage, with its strange language ('The hunted deludes himself into thinking that he is the hunter. He does not hear his own cry of pain. When he digs into his own flesh he thinks he is giving himself pleasure') is heavy with Schopenhauerian language (compare the philosopher's 'The hungry wolf buries its teeth in the flesh of the deer with the same necessity with which the stone falls to the ground, without the possibility of knowledge that it is the mauled as well as the mauler'). See Beckett 1994, 80.

4 Donington 1976, 19.

5 Plato often spoke of poets producing their works of art out of a sort of madness. See especially *Apology* 22b–c, *Ion* 5346b–e, and *Phaedrus* 249d–e.

6 *Über Staat und Religion*, written in 1864 for King Ludwig II. Wagner discusses *Wahn* as the irrational but potentially creative response his new patron derives from listening to his music, and adds that the true artist, exemplified in his Hans Sachs, can even use *Wahn* to bring order to a world thrown by unreason into disorder.

7 *The Interpretation of Dreams* was to be the title Freud gave his breakthrough work. But of course it is Schopenhauer who is the motivating force here: he thought that the dreams experienced just before waking, formed deep in the unconscious mind but still accessible

to the waker, were closely connected to artistic processes. See
Warrack 1994, 33–5.

8   This is one of the scenes, found in every Wagner work, in which a
character remains silent and is provided with an opportunity for
mime. Compare Senta's long silence in Act II of *Der Fliegende
Holländer*, Elisabeth's in Act III of *Tannhäuser*, Elsa's in Act I of
Lohengrin, Brünnhilde's on being awakened in the *Ring*, Isolde's at
the start of *Tristan*, and especially Kundry's in the last act of *Parsifal*, where she is on stage for almost an hour, sings only two words,
and in most performances makes a profound impression by gestures and movements alone.

9   Here Wagner makes charming use of the legend of St Crispin, the
patron saint of shoemakers, whose praises are sung in *Die Meistersinger*'s final scene. In the legend, which survives in different traditions in France and England, the humble Crispin fell in love with
the Princess Ursula, daughter of the Emperor Maximinus, when he
delivered a pair of shoes to her castle. They had little chance of seeing each other again, but she cunningly pretended that the shoes
pinched, and he was summoned to her side and thus enabled, not
just to stroke her foot, but to propose to and win her.

10 See Beckett 1994, 79. Beckett's article is beyond praise for its clarity
and insight.

11 The chromatic *Tristan und Isolde* and the diatonic *Die Meistersinger*
were written back-to-back, and are in many ways counterparts,
perhaps the most remarkable counterparts in art since Plato's spiritual *Phaedo* and the next dialogue he wrote, the erotic *Symposium*.
The measure of Wagner can be taken if *Tristan* and *Die Meistersinger* are seen, with all the differences between them, as com-
plementary statements about renunciation. 'Tristan and Isolde
renounce the world for their love's sake,' writes Peter Wapnewski
(1986, 74), and 'Hans Sachs renounces love for the world's sake –
that is, for the sake of his own particular world, the world of art.'

12 One of the most touching of many personal testaments to the guidance and support that the character of Hans Sachs can offer in
dealing with human problems is this from bass baritone Giorgio
Tozzi: 'Sachs came into my life when I needed him. I was going

through a crisis – mental, emotional, career, everything. That's when you need strong people. I had friends and a strong wife, but I drew more wisdom from Sachs than from any of them. Only because he was a friend did I have the nerve to do my first performance, which happened to be on the air, after being ill through all the rehearsals and missing performances' (Jenkins 1968, 26). Tozzi's Met broadcast, on 14 January 1967, was a revelation to me, as was his performance in the film made in Hamburg in 1970.

13 The speech, by far the most problematic in the opera, partly reflects the sentiments expressed in *What Is German?*, the 1865 essay Wagner sent to King Ludwig II: the German spirit, best seen in the life and work of Johann Sebastian Bach, will achieve greatness if it seeks what is noble and beautiful, not profit or military might. Sachs does not, however, speak with the essay's anti-democratic and anti-Semitic biases.

14 Many of the metaphorical patterns that follow were traced by Morse Peckham (1962, 258–9), who writes, 'To work it all out is a delightful – and instructive – exercise in literary interpretation.' I traced out the details independently of Peckham at about the same time, while teaching the patterns of imagery in the Odes of Horace.

15 In Wagner's earlier drafts of the Act III scene in Sachs's workshop, Walther's song told, in a fluid series of images, how as a youth he left home led by a white dove (perhaps an emblem of Goethe's 'eternal feminine') and how the dove brought him to the Tree of Life, caught a branch in its beak, and crowned his head with it. This was replaced in later drafts of the song with the more structurally useful idea of Eva in the *Abgesang* prefigured in the two *Stollen* as Eve in Paradise and the Muse of Parnassus. But the white dove in the first draft seems to have survived all the same, in this remark of Hans Sachs.

16 After the initial stanza used by Wagner in the opera, the poem, titled *Die Wittenbergisch Nachtigall*, goes on to attack the Catholic Church, its clergy, and its sale of indulgences. The historical Hans Sachs, who was deeply disturbed by the religious divisions in his Germany ('Wahn! Wahn!' indeed) was at first reprimanded by the city council of Nuremberg for writing the poem, but when it

became a rallying cry for the Reformation, there was no question
of censuring him.

17 The text and a translation are provided in the appendix.

18 The text and a translation (freely rendered from Wagner's elabo-
rately effusive verses) are provided in the appendix.

19 Donington 1976, 19. In a great passage in *The World as Will and Representation*, Schopenhauer wrote that 'the doctrine of original sin
(affirmation of the will) ... is really the great truth which constitutes
the kernel of Christianity,' and that 'what the Christian church very
appropriately called *new birth*, and the knowledge from which it
springs, *the effect of divine grace* ... is for us an expression of the
freedom of the will.' (The parentheses and emphases here are
Schopenhauer's.) Also pertinent is the remark Wagner made to
Lizst when he read the Schopenhauer passage: 'I have found your
own thoughts here. Although you express them differently because
you are religious, I nevertheless know that you think exactly the
same thing.' Both quotations are cited in Beckett 1994, 80–1.

20 See especially Wagner's 1854 letter to August Roeckel as quoted in
Donington 1974 [1963], 260: 'In the end, woman suffering and vol-
untarily sacrificing herself is the real and conscious redeemer; for
indeed love is the "eternal feminine."' Donington adds, 'If we cannot understand this final theme of redemption, we cannot understand Wagner. It was his life-long preoccupation, almost from the
beginning.'

21 About his visit to Venice with the Wesendoncks in 1861, Wagner
wrote in *Mein Leben* (*My Life*, 667): 'Titian's *Assumption of the Virgin*
in the great hall of the Doges made a most exalting impression on
me, so that by this inspiration I found my old creative powers
awakening within me with almost their original primordial power.
I decided to write *Die Meistersinger*.' (Wagner actually saw the
painting in the Accademia, not in the Doge's Palace; he corrected
that mistake later.) Some critics have questioned the truth of Wagner's account, citing a letter he wrote to Mathilde Wesendonck
later that same year, in which he actually apologizes for his *lack* of
enthusiasm for the paintings he saw in Venice. But there is almost
always an element of truth in Wagner's 'fabrications' in *Mein*

Leben. (Others are the 'vision' of La Spezia, where, Wagner said, the opening measures of *Das Rheingold* flooded in on him while he was lying in a semi-conscious state, and the *Parsifal* sketch that, he recorded, came to him in his garden on a beautiful morning that, it only occurred to him later, was the morning of Good Friday.) John Deathridge rightly says that the 'poetic truth' of these fabricated memories 'can sometimes be more instructive for our understanding of the dramatic works than sober, empirical exactitude would have been. Understanding the paths along which Wagner's imagination set off is more important than correcting conscious or unconscious inaccuracies' (Deathridge and Dahlhaus 1984, 91). It is, accordingly, quite possible that Wagner was inspired by Titian's *Assumption*, not just to commence work on the music for *Die Meistersinger*, but eventually to introduce Marian elements into the text of Walther's Prize Song when he revised that text four years later.

22 In the last year of his life Wagner saw the painting again, and Cosima wrote, 'It makes a glorious impression ... The glowing head of the Virgin Mary recalls to him his idea of the sexual urge, this unique and mighty force, now freed of all desire, the Will enraptured and redeemed' (*Cosima's Diaries* 1990, entry for Tuesday, 25 April 1882). Note the association of the Virgin Mary with the perennial Wagnerian theme of the redemptive woman (see note 19 above). If the 'Will' that Wagner found 'enraptured and redeemed' in the glowing head of Titian's Virgin Mary is the 'Wille' of Schopenhauer's thought – and there is every reason to believe that it is – then we have support for finding Marian resonances in the 'Huld-geboren' and 'Ruhm-erkoren' in the final version of the Prize Song: when Walther sings of Eva first as Eve in the Garden of Eden, then as the Muse of Parnassus, and finally as the Virgin Mary, all of Nuremberg is 'enraptured and redeemed,' cleansed of its *Wahn*, freed from the savage force of *Wille*.

CHAPTER FOUR   Controversies

1 Lucy Beckett, 1994, 69.
2 See Vaget 2002, 193.

3 These performances, ordered by Hitler himself, were actually
   scorned by Nazi officers and common soldiers, who had to be
   rounded up in their barracks and beer halls and ordered into the
   opera house. Heinz Tietjen, general manager at Bayreuth, said that
   'in reality the leading party officials throughout the Reich were
   hostile to Wagner.' The *Ring* was regarded by Alfred Rosenberg, the
   Nazi's influential racial theorist, as 'neither heroic nor Germanic.'
   Frederick Spotts, historian of the Bayreuth festival, records that
   Parsifal was banned throughout Germany in 1939, and Brian
   Magee notes that 'performances of Wagner's operas in Germany
   did not increase in frequency under the Nazis, they diminished,
   and very markedly.' See Magee 2000, 365–6.
4 Though Nurembergers are still thought by people outside of Germany to have been dyed-in-the-wool Nazis from the start, Berger
   (1998, 204) notes that 'after the fateful 1935 election of Hitler as
   Chancellor of Germany, seventy thousand Nurembergers rallied
   in the streets against National Socialism.' Other German cities
   vied for the 'honour' of being the showcase of Nazism, but not
   Nuremberg.
5 It is a distinct and usually overlooked possibility that the lines,
   addressed to Walther in the opera, may have been intended primarily for King Ludwig II, who invited Wagner to the royal box for
   the premiere, and thanked him afterwards in a letter signed
   'Walther.' Ludwig was troubled at the time that his Bavaria might
   be annexed by Austria.
6 *Wälsch*, the word translated here as 'foreign,' originally referred to
   any neighbouring tribe. For Anglo-Saxons, it meant the Celtic
   tribes in the British Isles; on the continent it came to mean Latin as
   opposed to Germanic, and even 'foreign' in the sense of 'incompre-
   hensible.' (The historical Sachs used it thus in one of his poems.) In
   any case it did not mean 'Jewish.' See Warrack 1994, 164. In the
   opera the word is almost certainly intended to mean 'French': the
   Franco-Prussian War was an impending threat at the time of the
   Meistersinger premiere, and in two pamphlets, 'What Is German?'
   (1865) and 'German Art and German Politics' (1867), Wagner
   argued for a regeneration of German 'folk spirit' after the French

dominance of culture and politics following on Napoleon's conquests.

7 It might be necessary today to observe that the Holy Roman Empire – which was, as the saying has it, neither holy, nor Roman, nor an empire – was ruled mainly by Germans for five centuries. Medieval Nuremberg was an imperial free city, a storehouse of imperial treasures, and in many ways the capital of the Holy Roman Empire. Hans Sachs's final address can only be properly understood if one knows that in his day the Empire was in danger of going under, and that its last remnants would finally be swept away by Napoleon and his French armies.

8 The sixteenth-century mastersingers traced their origin back to 'twelve great masters,' including Walther von der Vogelweide; the number twelve was probably chosen with the twelve apostles in mind. See Vazsonyi 2002, 8.

9 Porter 1978, 244–5.

10 Mann 1933, 141,

11 Warrack 1994, p. 31. Wagner actually struck out the couplet 'Rühme der deutsche Krieger / Besiegter oder Sieger' (Honour the German warrior, whether conquered or victorious').

12 See Kupfer 2002, 40.

13 Rosen 2006, 48.

14 Virgil's lines (*Aeneid* 6.847–53) are, like Wagner's, a peroration solemnly addressed to a single character by a father-figure, and are concerned with art, race, and military might: 'Other races, I firmly believe, will be more skilful, hammering out bronze statues so that they even seem to breathe. Others will plead causes more eloquently, and measure with instruments the paths of heavenly bodies, and predict the risings of the stars. But you, O Roman, remember to rule peoples with empire (that will be your art), to impose civilization after making peace, to show mercy to the conquered and to wage total war on the unconquered.'

It is worth noting, in the face of those who regard these lines as bombastic, that the arts in which 'others' are said to be more skilled – portrait sculpture, oratory, and science – were actually among the highest achievements of ancient Rome. What Virgil is

saying is that good Roman government through centuries of war
and peace would be a greater accomplishment still. And what
Wagner is saying in his controversial lines is that, for the survival
of civilization, art is more important than military might.

15 Herman Prey, in his remarkable portrayal of Beckmesser at
Bayreuth in the 1970s, 'illustrated a human side of the Nuremberg
town clerk, making him a fussy pedant who takes himself so seriously that his downfall becomes poignant rather than parodistic'
(Freeman 1998, 117). Nor was Prey alone in his portrayal. Joseph
Horowitz, at a Bayreuth symposium on Wagner and the Jews,
argued persuasively that Beckmesser and those other characters
thought to be anti-Semitic caricatures – Alberich, Mime, and Kundry – are in fact compassionate portraits, and he based his argu-
ment largely on performances past and present. See Horowitz
1998, 17.

16 It is worth noting that the humiliation of Malvolio by the other
characters in Shakespeare's *Twelfth Night* is, even within the broad
compass of comedy, much more reprehensible than the humiliation of Beckmesser, or rather the humiliation Beckmesser brings
upon himself, in *Die Meistersinger*. Malvolio's punishment is
almost completely unmotivated and gratuitous: of all the characters only the Clown has a real grievance – and that is merely that
Malvolio had called him 'a barren rascal' in front of his ladyship.
None of the others can say why they feel obliged to torment him.
Mark Van Doren (1955, 139–40) says, 'Doubtless they have never
thought it out. They only know that the sight of Malvolio, like the
sound of his voice, threatens death to their existence. His own
existence somehow challenges their right to be freely what they
are. He is of a new order – ambitious, self-contained, cold and
intelligent, and dreadfully likely to prevail. That is why Sir Toby
and his retinue hate him.' *Die Meistersinger* no less than *Twelfth
Night* deserves to be read in the comic tradition it represents.

17 'So ganz boshaft doch keinen ich fand. / Er halt's auf die Länge
nicht aus. / Vergeudet mancher oft viel Verstand, / doch hält er
auch damit Haus: / Die Schwache Stunde kommt für jeden; / da
wird er dumm und lässt mit sich reden.'

18 Adorno 1981, 23. The twentieth-century Marxist social philoso-
    pher and musicologist thought Wagner's music reactionary and
    dilettantish (especially when compared to Schoenberg's) and
    Wagner's texts a bourgeois flight from reality. A formidable
    polemicist, Adorno nonetheless deliberately and almost consis-
    tently misread Wagner's intentions and his achievement. In his
    remarks on *Die Meistersinger*, he spoke of Magdalene as an object
    of 'ridicule,' of Walther as hoping 'to reestablish the old feudal
    immediacy, as opposed to the bourgeois division of labour
    enshrined in the guilds,' of the mastersingers as characterized
    by 'dishonesty,' of Wagner's Nuremberg as 'fraudulent,' of the
    theatergoer enjoying the Act II riot as 'really gloating at a mini-
    ature foretaste of the violence to come,' of the quintet in Act III
    as a moment wherein Wagner's 'creativity dries up.' The barbs
    directed by Adorno at Wagner's other works are even wider of the
    mark, and his attempted philippic ultimately descends to the level
    of an indigestible diatribe. Most of the ideas of the anti-*Meister-
    singer* coterie are offshoots of Adornian spleen. The members
    should be reminded that, a quarter-century after his hypercritical
    In Search of Wagner, Adorno published a more balanced assess-
    ment, *Wagner's Topicality.*
19 This has been reasonably established in two research projects, con-
    ducted independently of each other, by Dina Porat and Saul
    Friedländer. See Vaget 2002, 194.
20 This has been established beyond any reasonable doubt by David
    B. Dennis after an exhaustive search through a veritable mountain
    of material. See Dennis 2002, 98–119. He concludes that *Die Meis-
    tersinger* 'was primarily utilized as an icon of cultural conservatism
    rather than as propaganda for fomenting racist hatred.'
21 Even Adorno, who first mentioned the Grimm story in connection
    with Wagner's anti-Semitism, did not connect it with Beckmesser.
    See Adorno 1981, 21, and Vaget 1995a, 36.
22 The unconfirmed newspaper report (mentioned in Cosima Wag-
    ner's diary entry for 14 March 1870, but nowhere else) that Jews in
    Vienna hissed at Beckmesser's serenade thinking it a parody of
    their music was written by an extremist in the Wagner camp who

seems to have been spreading what was, despite Cosima's qualms, only a rumour. See Grey 2002, 184–5. There is, however, little question that Wagner, certain that *Die Meistersinger* would be a triumph, intentionally republished his 'Judaism in Music' for the premiere – and *that* was what the audience was hissing at.

23 Another coterie member says of Beckmesser's defeat that he 'is beaten and expelled, and his public execution is sublimated into the horrific phantasy of ritual exclusion' (quoted in Vaget 2002, 204–5). Beckmesser is indeed beaten in the riot that ends Act II of the opera, but then so is virtually every other man in Wagner's Nuremberg. And be it noted, he is beaten only by David, and beaten not because he was an object of scorn but because David had seen him serenading his sweetheart, Magdalene, thinking she was Eva. Beckmesser is neither 'expelled' nor in any way executed in Act III. Wagner says that 'he rushes away furiously and disappears into the crowd.' (And what, one may ask in any case, is a 'horrific phantasy of ritual exclusion' supposed to mean?) Most outrageous of all is the remark of yet another coterie member (quoted in Brockmann 2006, 110) that 'Beckmesser has literally "undergone ritual circumcision"'!

24 See *Opera*, August 1995, 906, n. 10; *Opera Now*, November/December 1997, 103; and *BBC Music Magazine*, August 2003, 89. Note that these *recusationes* were made in popular magazines, not in scholarly journals. In the face of criticism by the philosopher Bryan Magee, all that the rueful recusant in the BBC magazine can say in his own defence is, 'What is it with philosophers?' As recently as 2006 he was still charging, but with a mite of caution, that 'some' suspected a 'dark underside' in *Die Meistersinger*.

25 Hans Rudolph Vaget has kept his sanity and sense of humour while fending off what he calls a 'mutual admiration and quotation society' whose members are at best a 'representative example of that post-modern, "new historical" practice of literary scholarship ... characterized by a strategic shift of emphasis away from the text and towards the context as the privileged generator of signification.' That is to say, they are deconstructionists (Vaget 1995b, 4 and 8). Bryan Magee too has remained, in the face of the opposi-

tion, a gentleman, but a rather sad one: 'We are confronted, then, with a considerable and still growing body of literature in which the truth of many untruths is assumed.' For anyone disturbed by the untruths, Magee's full comment (Magee 2000, 368–79) is essential reading. Perhaps the whole regrettable controversy has been necessary in order to set the record straight on how much – that is to say, how little – Wagner may be held responsible for National Socialism.

26 Levin, 'Music from the Depths,' an occasional piece in *The London Times*, ca. 1993.

BIBLIOGRAPHY

Adorno, Theodor. 1981 [1952]. *In Search of Wagner*. Trans. Rodney Livingstone. London: NLB.

Beckett, Lucy. 1994. 'Sachs and Schopenhauer.' In Warrack 1994, 66–82.

Berger, William. 1998. *Wagner without Fear*. New York: Vintage Books.

Borchmeyer, Dieter. 1992 [1986]. 'The Question of Anti-Semitism.' Trans. Stewart Spenser. In Müller and Wapnewski 1992, 166–85.

– 2003 [2002]. *Drama and the World of Richard Wagner*. Trans. Daphne Ellis. Princeton: Princeton University Press.

Brockmann, Stephen. 2006. *Nuremberg: The Imaginary Capital*. Rochester, NY: Camden House.

Dahlhaus, Carl. 1979 [1971]. *Richard Wagner's Music Dramas*. Cambridge: Cambridge University Press.

Deathridge, John, and Carl Dahlhaus. 1984. *The New Grove Wagner*. New York: Norton & Company.

Dennis, David B. 2002. 'The Most German of All German Operas: *Die Meistersinger* through the Lens of the Third Reich.' In Vazsonyi 2002, 98–119.

Donington, Robert. 1974 [1963]. *Wagner's 'Ring' and Its Symbols*. London: Faber and Faber.

– 1976. 'Wagner and *Die Meistersinger*.' In *Opera News*, 17 April, 18–19.

Freeman, John W. 1998. Obituary for Herman Prey. In *Opera News*, September 1998, 117.

Grey, Thomas S. 2002. 'Masters and Their Critics: Wagner, Hanslick, Beckmesser, and *Die Meistersinger*.' In Vazsonyi 2002, 165–89.

Horowitz, Joseph. 1998. 'Nothing Approaching Caricature.' In *Times Literary Supplement*, 21 August, 16–17.

Höyng, Peter. 2002. 'http://*worldwidewagner*.richard.de: An Interview with the Composer concerning History, Nation, and *Die Meistersinger*.' In Vazsonyi 2002, 120–42.

Jenkins, Speight. 1968. 'At Home with Sachs.' In *Opera News*, 28 December, 26.

John, Nicholas, ed. 1983. *The Mastersingers of Nuremberg*. New York: Riverrun Press.

Kupfer, Harry. 2002. 'We Must Finally Stop Apologizing for *Die Meistersinger*!' In Vazsonyi 2002, 39–49.

Lee, M. Owen. 1998. *Wagner: The Terrible Man and His Truthful Art*. Toronto: University of Toronto Press.

– 2002 [1995]. *First Intermissions*. New York: Amadeus Press.

Levin, Bernard. ca 1993. 'Music from the Depths.' In *The London Times*.

Magee, Bryan. 1988 [1968]. *Aspects of Wagner*. Oxford: Oxford University Press.

– 2000. *The Tristan Chord*. New York: Henry Holt and Company.

Mann, Thomas. 1933. 'The Sorrows and Grandeur of Richard Wagner.' In *Thomas Mann: Pro and Contra Wagner*, ed. Allan Blunden. London: Faber and Faber, 1985.

Matthews, Roland. 1983. '"My most genial creation."' In John 1983, 7–14.

McFarland, Timothy. 1983. 'Wagner's Nuremberg.' In John 1983, 27–34.

Müller, Ulrich, and Peter Wapnewski. 1992 [1986]. *Wagner Handbook*. Trans. John Deathridge. Cambridge, Mass.: Harvard University Press.

Newman, Ernest. 1949. *Wagner Nights*. London: Putnam & Company.

– 1976 [1937–47]. *The Life of Richard Wagner*. 4 vols. Cambridge: Cambridge University Press.

Peckham, Morse. 1962. *Beyond the Tragic Vision*. New York: George Braziller.

Pleasants, Henry. 1950. 'Eduard Hanslick.' In *Eduard Hanslick: Music Criticisms 1846–99*. Harmondsworth: Penguin Books.

Porter, Andrew. 1978. *Music of Three Seasons: 1974–1977*. New York: Farrar, Straus, Giroux.

Rosen, Charles. 2006. 'From the Troubadours to Sinatra: Part II.' In *New York Review of Books*, 9 March 2006, 44–8.

Spencer, Stewart. 2000. *Wagner Remembered*. London: Faber and Faber.

Tanner, Michael. 1997. *Wagner*. London: Flamingo.

Vaget, Hans Rudolf. 1994. 'Reply.' In *The German Quarterly* 67.3 (Summer), 408–10.

– 1995a. 'Sixtus Beckmesser – A Jew in the Brambles?' *The Opera Quarterly* 12 (Autumn), 35–46.

– 1995b. 'Imaginings.' *Wagner Notes* 18 (December), 4–9.

– 2002. 'Du warst mein Feind von je: The Beckmesser Controversy Revisited.' In Vazrsonyi 2002, 190–208.

Van Doren, Mark. 1955 [1939]. *Shakespeare*. New York: Doubleday & Company.

Vazsonyi, Nicholas, ed. 2002. *Wagner's Meistersinger: Performance, History, Representation*. Rochester: University of Rochester Press.

Wagner, Cosima. 1978, 1990. *Cosima Wagner's Diaries*. Trans. Geoffrey Skelton. 2 vols. New York: Harcourt Brace Jovanovich.

Wagner, Richard. 1983. *My Life (Mein Leben)*. Ed. Mary Whittall, trans. Andrew Gray. Cambridge: Cambridge University Press.

Wapnewski, Peter. 1986. 'The Operas as Literary Works.' Trans. Peter Palmer. In Müller and Wapnewski 1992, 73–83.

Warrack, John. 1994. *Richard Wagner: Die Meistersinger von Nürnberg*. Cambridge: Cambridge University Press.

INDEX OF NAMES

A special thank you to my editor recommended to me as a "crackerjack editor" Mary Beth Baker Giltner of the "Our Sunday Visitor".

Her deep understanding of the Catholic faith made all the difference. Her competence and recommendations as an editor/consultant was seamless. Her great love for God and the Church made the book a natural fit. She calls this book inspiring and contagious.

Thank you, Mary Beth for your God given talent and grace.

Thank you to Father Marc Roselli, SJ for hours of edits and reflections. Marc you are a gifted teacher with a heart for your students and parishioners. You have a gift for spiritual direction, indeed.

Thank you to Father Binoy Davis, Parochial Vicar at St. Matthew's Church, Charlotte, North Carolina. You and your church are an inspiration to me. Thank you for reviewing the book.

Thank you to Father Dennis Mende for being our shepherd and sharing your reflections on parts of the book.

Thank you Kathleen McGough Johnson for your input in writing this book, and the many enjoyable hours we travelled to parishes finding answers to our quests.

CONTENTS

PREFACE

*"Who is going to save our Church? Not our bishops,
not our priests and religious. It is up to you, the
people. You have the minds, the eyes, and the ears
to save the Church. Your mission is to see that
your priests act like priests, your bishops act like
bishops, and your religious act like religious."*

Archbishop Fulton J. Sheen
(speech to the Knights of Columbus, June 1972)

F ollowing the scandals that erupted in 2018 in the
Diocese of Buffalo, New York and the Grand Jury
report that was released in Pennsylvania, the sex
scandals in our Church once again became a public, and
troubling, topic of conversation. The Church was in grave
turmoil, particularly in the Diocese of Buffalo. My friend
Kathleen McGough Johnson and I responded to Dr. John
Hurley, the president of Canisius College in Buffalo, after
he wrote an article in the *Buffalo News* in response to the
scandals. His letter announced that it was the laity that
would restore the Church. Both of us felt called to respond,
and so we became two of the first thirty people to organize

the Movement to Restore Trust (MRT), which still existed at the time of writing this book. This organization is made up of many devout Catholics with wonderful skills and experience, and they moved quickly.

Listening sessions were organized in the diocese by MRT. These listening sessions were set up to listen to individual Catholics in parishes that had issues with the Church and had experienced some part of the scandals. The stories in the sessions were compelling, disturbing, and heartbreaking. Overall, it was a frightening experience that stirred anger, dismay, disappointment, a deep sadness. For the first time, I felt shame for my church. Kathleen and I said to each other, *We have to do something. We're going to lose the Church as we know it, just like they lost the Catholic Church in Europe when all of this happened ten years ago.* I can attest to this, as I had personally witnessed it upon my bi-annual family visits to the Netherlands. There will be more on this in the final chapter of the book. So our big question became, "What is a parish?"

What makes up a parish? How do we get a parish strong again and better than ever? Where are the good ones? And so we decided to formulate a research questionnaire based on observation, which we used for **visiting and analyzing 25 percent of the parishes** in the Diocese of Buffalo. Each parish had a file with a questionnaire comprising 165 factors for analysis. Each Sunday at a different diocesan parish, we interviewed parishioners and pastors. We spoke to most pastors for one to two hours. Our quest was to learn what the essential elements of a strong Catholic parish were, and who does it well? We created and conducted our project on our own, which took a year and a half.

We felt conflicted by the concerns of resolving sex abuse litigation with the need to immediately address the pleas from the laity for reform in the Church as a whole. The pressure for Vatican action was mounting. In the summer of 2019, Pope Francis urged calm, quiet discourse. Subsequently, Bishop Richard J. Malone of Buffalo announced he was taking early retirement after much encouragement from the faithful of his diocese. Chancery staff began to leave, and additionally, the seminary was forced to close. The Child Victims Act of August 2019 allowed one year for survivors of past sexual abuse beyond statute of limitations to file their claims going back several decades.

Meanwhile, in our own parish, Saints Peter and Paul Church in Jamestown, New York, the pews were empty in the center of the church. People were leaving the parish in droves, just as was happening in many other Catholic parishes in the Diocese of Buffalo. Collections dropped by 30 to 50 percent. People were voting with their wallets and with their feet. Kathleen and I were not discouraged but increasingly aware of the trend. The more we researched, the more we understood. Even our own pastor, Father Dennis Mende, called for Bishop Malone to resign because the people had lost faith in him.

In spite of the many hardships and scandals we faced in our Church, Kathleen and I felt certain that hope and healing were possible.

The first question: What went wrong to result in extreme turmoil for the diocese? With zero tolerance advocated and the Charter for the Protection of Children and Young People by the US Conference of Catholic Bishops of 2002 in place, what hit the media that the concerned Catholic did not know about and created a tsunami in the parishes and for the chancery?

The second question we asked was: If the purpose of the Church is to save souls, why were pews emptying, and where did we go wrong? Are people coming to church as consumers, meaning simply to attend church, get out the door quickly, and remain minimally involved in church? Or merely attending church with no deep spirituality which is called religiosity? It takes much more to grow in spirituality into a mature Christian witnessing Christ to others. For God never changes, but how we connect with God does.

A third question for our mission came out of our own Catholic concern to grow the Church for Christ. Is not the ultimate purpose of church to become a community of disciples of Jesus Christ? In Matthew 28:16–20 and Luke 14:26–27, Jesus calls on his followers "to make disciples of and baptize all nations in the name of the Father, and of the Son and of the Holy Spirit."

How well are we doing at this in the Catholic Church? My brother Mike left the Catholic Church and now belongs to an evangelical church. This is not uncommon for Catholics—in fact, 40 percent of Catholics (Giesler, 2013) who leave the Catholic Church end up in evangelical churches. Well, Mike continues to ask me the same question over the years: "Just how many people have you brought to Jesus?" See for Mike, the fruit of the Spirit is witnessed by the number of people he brings to Christ. This is called discipleship and evangelization, and we as Christians are commissioned by Christ to bring the good news to all people and to make disciples going out to all the ends of the earth. If we are not helping people to deepen their faith, we are not fulfilling the commission that Christ has given us.

The first chapter of the book Culture Eats Strategy for Breakfast relays the results of the MRT listening sessions which describe the Catholic culture today. The following chapters are the results of our study on the parishes. The solutions to the problems discussed in the book address the results of both studies. The book is not an exposé on the sex scandals but an exposé on the crisis in the church and offering real solutions to the problems in our parishes.

This book will be an exploration on how we can improve and focus on the worship service, on discipleship, on evangelizing, and how we can draw closer together through fellowship by studying how others are working at it successfully in the American Catholic Church.

The Catholic Church has existed since the time of Christ—for over 20 centuries. It still exists, although broken. Let us explore the elements of how to rebuild the Catholic parish so that we may heal and make the whole Church better than it has ever been in the last 2,000 years. We can do this. Be encouraged to give your life, your heart, to Jesus and help save the Church because He saved you first.

Remember, God does not change; we do. Let us find our way to worship with one voice and be filled with the joy that only God can give. Let us address the grievances and heal through repentance and reconciliation. Let us build fellowship and restore trust.

CHAPTER 1

CULTURE EATS STRATEGY
FOR BREAKFAST

Somewhere during my planning education, I heard it said, "Culture eats strategy for breakfast." When thinking about the Catholic Church, this means you can create all kinds of strategies to grow the Church, but if you are not dealing with the culture first, the strategies will not be successful in achieving your goal. Well, we all know that we need a good breakfast to start out, so let us begin.

When we with MRT began our half-day Listening Sessions with the parishes in the Diocese of Buffalo, we heard grievous complaints about the state of the Church. Essentially the issues/complaints were the same in each parish. As we listened carefully and actively, we realized that all the issues and complaints we heard related to the culture that now exists in our parishes. In all likelihood, this same culture also exists in other dioceses. We must address these cultural issues for new strategies to work rebuilding parishes.

This chapter is divided into three sections, what's problematic about church culture, each one focusing on a different issue that is part of the culture in today's Catholic churches. These three sections are:

1. Kids who are our future

2. Priests who are our sacramental Christ figures

3. Adults who form the laity of the parish

1. KIDS TRULY ARE OUR FUTURE IN THE PARISH

Laity mentioned concern over the American culture of violence and sex in music, videos, and games and the influence on their children. Also, pointing out distractions of school sports and events interfering with Church activities. Our parishes need to make a concerted effort to work with these concerns and time tables.

One felt the grief as parents voiced these concerns. Kids were not coming to Mass or even to religious education when they were older. Parishioners were frustrated by the lack of youth programs, and the lackluster leadership in religious education. Parishioners felt that their parishes offered little to no support of the child's spiritual development, resulting in shortsightedness for future parish growth. The result was the abandonment of worship by young people and their families. They simply stopped going to Mass.

The problems voiced on the religious education programs were multiple. Programs lacked substance, to the point of insulting the intelligence of children; they lacked spiritual guidance and inspiration; children could not identify with leadership; and leadership offered no worthy takeaways for students. The litany from parents at the listening sessions went on. Kids did not even know what a mortal sin was or that it needed to be confessed before receiving the Body and Blood of Christ. High school kids could not recite the Ten Commandments. They simply had not been taught! Children had forgotten or never knew that it was a mortal sin to miss Sunday Mass. If children were taught the Catechism (not understood if this meant the Baltimore Catechism or the Catechism promulgated under John Paul II), they would know why they were created and would feel they had a purpose in life. It was proposed to include the Catechism in faith formation.

Most parishes we visited did not have a youth group, providing young people an opportunity for Catholic fellowship to grow in the Word, to disciple, and learn to evangelize.

2. Priests as sacramental Christ figures

The issues

Listening sessions produced several important and helpful comments. Parishioners told us it was difficult "to look at accused priests with trust and respect." They wanted transparency when allegations were made so "laity could" make sure the priests were handled with appropriate and effective means. Some questioned if measures could be taken to allow priests to marry or, permitting female deacons and female priests. Perhaps laity should be involved in appointing and choosing bishops at the local level although this is not a democratic feature of the Church but hierarchical.

People also felt that their priests did not talk enough about crisis with their flocks. Why did priests not talk to the people about the scandals arising in the Church? They seemed to ignore the flock's pain over the descriptions of the sex scandals in the media. Priests were not talking about the Sacraments or encouraging confession from the pulpit. Why were priests not calling on people to become involved in a ministry or share talents and show them how to do it?

There was worry about bankruptcy and that it may force parishes to close, affecting staff pensions and threatening schools and ministries with closure.

Why were priests dismissed from the clerical state when found guilty as charged, but not sent to jail? There was a strong sentiment that the Church needed to be purged of the "lavender mafia" and new principles put in place to support celibacy and the other vows that priests take. This was the opposite of comments on allowing priests to marry.

And lastly voiced, true change has to allow accountability and transparency to balance the "company" or "boys' club" protecting the clergy.

Advice from the laity

The Listening Sessions continued with comments of advice from the laity. The Church needs a process of transparency with zero tolerance for abuse. Abuse must be treated as a crime: Simply call the police immediately when a credible allegation was heard repeatedly. The opposite concern was heard in that should the allegation be erroneous, it would cause irreparable damage to the priest. Therefore, local law enforcement should not be involved until there is confirmation of a crime committed.

Screening of the candidates to the seminary needed to be revamped, and there should be a policy in place to prevent the gay pipeline from happening again. (This refers to a time in the 1990s and the first decade of this century, and some say even today when gay seminarians discharged from the South American seminaries were recruited by houses of vocation discernment in New Jersey and New York. The purpose was to increase ordinations.) The laity believed, To allow candidates of this nature into the priesthood is like "putting a bear in a honey shop," another disgruntled person advised. On the other hand, a seminary candidate willing to abide by the rules and vows should be able to devote his life to priesthood. Two standards cannot exist spoiling it for others willing to remain celebate.

Some attendees expressed difficulty understanding how such a large population of priests with this proclivity, some say as high as 40 percent, were allowed to consecrate the bread and wine. It seemed the trend had been allowed because so many hundreds of priests left their vocation after Vatican II. Some wondered if the practice of priestly celibacy should be abandoned.

RESTORING TRUST IN THE CATHOLIC PARISH

Many felt that placing priests on a pedestal blinded parishioners to the transgressions of the perpetrators. These transgressions committed against families resulted in victim suicides, alcoholism, drug abuse, and family dysfunction. In several parishes, parishioners were angry that their trust in the priest and esteem had blinded them and as a result deeply harmed their child who depended on parents to protect them. Equally grievous was that the crime was perpetrated by their own shepherd of the flock. There needed to be counseling services and fellowship to help the abused families. Mentoring laity could become a new ministry in the parish.

Sometimes it appeared the priest did not want to share his power, but wanted to control everything, exhibiting an attitude that he knows best. Some who attended the Listening Sessions said that priests need support with friendship, respect, helpfulness, and encouragement.

Many priests did not know how to respond to the hurting members of their parishes. They did not know what to say or what to do to make up for the hurt the Church caused. This needed addressing. Some priests were dealing with their own concerns about mistreatment they received in public places, like being spat upon, shoved, glared at, and shunned.

Although the majority of abuses happened prior to 2002 with a minuscule number since (although even one is not acceptable) due to the strong procedures, education, and protocol in place, there was one underlying concern that set off the parishioners. It became apparent when the RICO investigation began. Racketeer Influenced and Corrupt Organization (RICO) are examining whether the clergy-at-large had known for decades about the abusers being shifted around the diocese following rehab which resulted in no apparent healing of the abuser. Until the RICO investigation is complete, there remains skepticism and distrust by the people.

As of this writing in 2020, a new bishop is being sought for the Diocese of Buffalo from outside of the diocese. Christ the King Seminary is closed indefinitely, and Bishop Malone resigned as requested.

3. ADULTS: OUR LAITY

The laity we met with considered this the worst crisis in the Church since the reformation started by Martin Luther 500 years ago, which resulted in ten of thousands of fragmented churches.

Many agreed that we have to rebuild the Church before we can convince the disenfranchised to want to come back; we have to be able to meet their needs. Among those who have stayed in the Church, there were feelings of betrayal and anger that were not being dealt with. There was fear in the air for the Church's future with no solutions or hope, just silence. It was suspected that more people will leave the Church out of frustration.

Many of the laity felt that there was a great need for more understanding of the Sacraments and what it means to be Catholic.

The abused and even disappointed and hurt bystanders needed counseling services and fellowship programs to help them mend.

The laity had more to say about the Catholic Church overall. Here were some of their concerns:

Catholics tended not to practice welcoming and building fellowship. Church should not be just limited to attendance at Sunday Mass. The Church needed to become more gratitude and joy-filled. The perception was that Church's main drive, especially coming from the diocese, is to raise money, not membership. There needed to be more focus on growing membership. The very small numbers in RCIA (Rite of Christian Initiation of Adults) and First Communion classes are examples of waning membership in parishes. Most Catholics we spoke with felt they have a membership to a church but do not feel a belonging. People had lost faith in the Church, and this was connected to the loss of faith in the Eucharist, loss of faith in priests and in confession, in the value of the Mass, in praying the Rosary, and sometimes believing in heaven and hell.

People did not want to commit to church ministries because there were too few to job-share. Many also had the attitude that "no one will come anyway."

The lay adults we met with felt they have no control or input to enact change. There was a feeling of hopelessness in the circumstances and in the future of the Church.

Church members expressed deep anger about the scandals and betrayal by the clergy as a whole. It was painful for the adult laity to recognize that the clergy-at-large knew about the replacement of treated clerics who were not cured or could not be cured, yet said nothing about it. The clergy seemed to be an old boys' club or "the company," and priests were company men. The laity in the diocese of Buffalo expressed deep anger and disappointment upon reading in the media that the chancery had been covering up replacement of questionable clerics for decades, even after zero tolerance had been put into place.

The laity felt betrayal. Their shepherds did not protect the flock. Church members expressed deep grief and sadness mixed with disappointment in the Catholic system, which was once so esteemed and trusted. Adults expressed shame for their church and vowed to withdraw support and even attendance.

There was worry about bankruptcy and that it may force churches to close and furthermore, affect staff pensions, and threatened the closing of schools and ministries.

There was fear that the diocese would follow the European country like the Netherlands, where 70 percent of the churches were closed after scandals hit over ten years ago. Today, in Europe, the churches remaining are poorly attended and almost exclusively by those over sixty-five years old. More on this in the final chapter of the book.

One thing we found in our listening sessions was need for testimonies to be shared in the Catholic Church to encourage others in faith-sharing. Catholics overall do not do this type of sharing, nor do they know how to evangelize.

The laity want priests to encourage involvement in ministry and to urge parishioners to share talents. The laity need the priests to show them how evangelize.

Lay people wanted a new Bible study model as in Bible studies for families to deepen and develop their faith together. Parishes would benefit from faith formation that unites families by helping them grow in faith together through a new Bible study model.

Many of the laypeople we spoke with expressed appreciation for the media that stopped the cover-up in the Church. The laity felt that now the Church needs a process of transparency with zero tolerance on abuse. Abuse must be treated as a crime. The police should be involved immediately upon confirmation of abuse by the Church. This was expressed several times. The opposite concern was voiced should the allegations be wrong, it would cause irreparable damage.

There was concern about how small parishes were going to survive the storm. Some of the parishes were very small, with the majority being elderly people and no one to help them with the church duties such as music, maintenance, Eucharistic ministry and visits to the sick, etc.

Lay people in many parishes was concerned that they heard the same homilies on the three-year Church calendar, which covers the whole Bible. Priests offer reflections on Scripture, and then repeat the homily every three years (although many priests vary the reflections from year to year). The laity suggested it would be more helpful to have a sermon so they can better relate Scripture to everyday issues. Family members are departing for evangelical churches that offer childcare during services, entertaining worship music, and a good sermon. Perhaps we should offer some of the same at Mass while keeping the reverence.

Adults felt they had lost their kids, as the parish was not meeting their church needs, and this caused problems in families. Most especially, there was concern regarding inadequate nourishment for their souls. Parents felt at a loss to know what to do and were frustrated with the Church. They had trusted the Church would do the job. The church had been well paid with tithings.

We were also told that there was not much sharing between nearby parishes. Parishes seemed to have an attitude of protectionism, guarding the congregation numbers and revenue by not sharing resources, programs, and know-how. Sometimes announcements and invites would not be shared with the other parishes. We did not know if on the part of the priest there was a concern with pew poaching. Communication through the bulletin and websites was outdated, unorganized, and unhelpful. Many thought that there was no plan or vision for their parish ... just the same old status quo.

†

To avoid ending this chapter on a negative note, we had to hear the parish voices in order to recommend changes appropriate and effective. I want the reader to know that I listened to the laity in the listening sessions. They were heard. When you base solutions on truth, you get somewhere. Silence is the worst response. Many readers will be able to relate to this chapter, however. It is time to get our heads out of the ground and into the heavens with prayers and proactive responses to restore trust, be spiritually fed, and reach out to the unchurched and the lost church.

To summarize, the culture in today's Catholic parishes must be addressed, in order for strategies to grow the Church. It must be taken into consideration when developing the vision, mission statement and motto for the parish.

*May God have mercy upon us and upon
the whole Church, we pray in the name
of Christ Jesus.*

CHAPTER 2

VISION, MISSION, STRATEGY

Chapter one was difficult, I am sure, for many of you to get through. However, it is vital to understand what problems and challenges are facing our parishes before we discuss resolving these enormous problems in our parishes. Next, we will talk about vision, mission statement, and strategy. By looking at how other exceptional parishes organize themselves and communicate with parishioners, we will see how they address issues, grow parishes, and are an encouragement to others by their modeling.

This chapter and those that follow are based on parish research done by Kathleen and me. We will be looking at the data from parishes in the diocese of Buffalo, as well as parishes in Pennsylvania, specifically Erie, Charlotte, North Carolina, and Houston, Texas.

This chapter and the following are based on a study Kathleen and I did. We visited forty parishes which is 25% of the Diocese of Buffalo and analyzed everything from appearance of the church, the Mass, the bulletin, website, ministries and so on. Since I am a planner by education and experience, the study is from a planning point of view. Our journey was to determine what makes some parishes vibrant and others not. A total of 165 factors were assessed and scored. This developed into rankings of five categories from parishes in a critical state or flat lining up to an exceptional parish.

VISION

Let's talk about vision. Why is vision important? This is important to understand because most of the parishes we met with did not have a vision statement.

As Joel A. Barker, a business developer and futurist, says, "Vision without action is merely a dream. Action without vision just passes the time" (*Oxford Essential Quotations*, Oxford University Press, 2016).

Nelson Mandela said, "Vision without action cannot change. Vision with action can change the world" (Nelson Mandela, *Long Walk to Freedom*).

Leadership in your parish is the capacity to translate vision into reality. "Where there is no vision, there is no hope," according to George Washington Carver, an Afro-American agricultural scientist (1880). And I am sure you have heard "without a vision, the people perish" (Proverbs 29:18).

In the book of Habakkuk (2:2) the prophet is annoyed with the Lord for not answering his questions and doing something about the wickedness and injustice in the community. The Lord answers, "Write the vision and make it plain." This is wonderful advice for any setting, and it allows the reader to run with it.

A Vision Statement is a destination, a fixed point to which we focus all our effort. A structured vision statement creates passion. It is a compass to the plan, while strategy is a route to get where we want to go. Strategy is the steps to reach the goal of the vision.

Steve Gilliland, former CEO of Southwest Airlines, said, "Without vision, you have no direction. Without direction, you have no purpose." Gordon B Hinckley said, "Work without vision is drudgery. Vision without work is just daydreaming." "It is just go along to get along."

Work plus vision creates change and allows you to achieve your dream, your vision for the parish.

MISSION STATEMENT

Of the many parishes we visited, only two had vision statements prominently in the bulletin. One was St. Joseph Bread of Life in Erie, Pennsylvania, and the other was St. John Vianney of Orchard Park, New York.

For Bread of Life, the vision and mission statement was written in the form of a prayer, located at the front of the bulletin just under the name of the parish. It was also on their website.

Seven parishes we visited had a mission statement and only two had a motto, but they did not have a vision or a mission statement at the front and center of their parish communication such as a bulletin and website. (If vision and mission statements existed somewhere in church documents, it did not count for our purpose because they need to be visible to everyone who visit the parish to serve their purpose.)

Mottos set the mindset of a group. The motto for Precious Blood parish in Angola, New York, read, "Let us do little things with great love." It is catchy and visual yet simple. It is also inspiring! This motto was located under the name of the parish on the front of the bulletin.

St. Gregory the Great's motto in Buffalo, New York, was in the same location on the bulletin, saying, "Parish community, living the gospel, in faith, in worship and in service." This is a soft version of a vision and mission statement combined but reads more like a motto.

St. Mary's of Swormville, New York, had their mission statement at the front of the bulletin under the name of the parish. It says, "We at St. Mary's Roman Catholic Church Parish follow the word of the Father, Son and Holy Spirit. We are dedicated to engaging our entire faith community in acts of worship, ministry, service and mission."

The vision is where you want to go, and the mission statement is a specific way to go about it, addressing how you are going to get there. It should be measurable for your ROI (Return on Investment) and accomplishment of goals, so you should be able to measure both the ROI and the goals. Otherwise, you only account for attendance and revenue, and that is not the true purpose of church.

When people are on the same page, it is easier to find volunteers and to get various kinds of participation. It is better to create your vision and mission statement than to copy others. In order to own it, to work at it, and to claim it as your own, it should come from your own minds and hearts in your parish. The vision and the mission statement becomes the basis for brainstorming the strategy. Otherwise you risk busy-ness, not productivity in the areas that count like spirituality, baptisms, number of ministries, size of the RCIA program, and support of parishioner needs and wants.

A parish should evaluate how well they lived out their mission statement every year to measure progress in parish development. The vision should be evaluated or measured every few years progress, to adjust in changes in membership, and goals.

St. Matthew's Church in Charlotte, North Carolina has a three year Pastoral Plan where goals are created by parish council, and reviewed by the Pastor and diocese. It could be spiritual development of Youth, campus expansion, pastoral care for sick or families etc. This is part of the vision and mission of the parish.

The motto of St. Matthew is "Connected in Christ, moved by the Spirit." The parish Mission Statement is "The Catholic community of St. Matthew seeks salvation through Jesus Christ. We are transformed through the sacraments, prayer, sacrifice, and acts of love and mercy. All are invited and welcomed to an encounter with the living God through our Catholic faith."

STRATEGY

It is highly recommended that a parish have a strategic planner take you through the exercises for visioning and strategic planning. This planner will be able to help you brainstorm and lead you in all the directions that are important for growing your parish, including worship, fellowship, discipleship, ministries, and evangelization. It is also an enjoyable experience. It gets people very engaged, excited, and motivated to help the parish grow. It also motivates parishioners to disciple or teach one another how to share the good news with the unchurched or with those who are thinking about coming back to the Catholic Church. It should focus first on the family.

It is recommended that the parish strategic planning session be done on a weekend, perhaps a Saturday or a Sunday afternoon, allowing for at least four hours to get through this planning exercise. We begin by sharing the ideal with the congregation. It would be a full day with lunch included. There should be a wide range of parishioners at this kind of session, not just board of trustees, parish life, and parish council. Make sure you have youth there and some representing all ministries in the parish. Having a large group of, say, 50 to 100 people is manageable. It can be organized so that everyone has the opportunity to provide input. It is also a great way to gather creative ideas and it may lead to various kinds of support for what the parish decides to do. Especially important in this exercise is the fun of it and the excitement. This is contagious. Not only will it remain with the participants, but it will energize those with whom they share.

Planning Session

We begin with sharing with the congregation the ideal because most people do not know what is out there. They are just mindful of their feelings that the parish is missing or lacking something. Some also carry an emotional burden from the scandals.

Next, we would take the parish through a list of improvements which the parish collected from one large parish meeting and from small group discussions. Members decide how they can contribute to the plan of action that the parish has created.

If this is done simultaneously with nearby parishes, a comprehensive plan can be created. For instance, if both parishes want a youth group, but one has an ideal location which the other parish does not or does not have enough of the other necessities, a combined effort creating one regional youth group may be the solution.

The information and the experience with all of the information at this type of planning session should be gathered into a document that is very well organized, understandable, and helpful. It is not a type of document that sits on a shelf, but calls for action and shows the way—the strategy to action. This type of exercise is very helpful for growing school numbers, growing parish numbers, growing ministries, growing financially, and perhaps most important of all, for growing disciples. All of us have been given the commission to go out and share the good news of Jesus Christ and to bring followers to Jesus.

O God have mercy upon us and upon the
whole church, we pray through Christ Jesus
who is, the truth, the way, and the life.

CHAPTER 3

STRATEGY FOR COMMUNICATION

I n the previous chapter, we focused on the critical need for vision and mission with a simple motto to clarify for the parishioner what we are about as a faith community. The staff and the faith community should know it from memory, know it in their hearts, and be inspired to follow through on the mission and vision. The focus for this chapter is to help parishioners follow that mission and vision. We want to establish great communication for parishioners, active laity, and staff. Picture a wheel. The cogs of the wheel of communication are the bulletin, the website, the organization contact chart, and the technology, including big screen, camera, video, sound, and music.

The communication strategy should be evaluated at least once per year. If this is not done, it will affect improvements, spiritual growth of parishioners, parish size, and personal satisfaction. This is where a skilled and dedicated administrator comes in. It may be the priest, deacon, parish administrator, parish life coordinator, or a similarly competent person with the right skills. It has to be someone who is not afraid to fire and hire, has HR competency, has experience, and has a heart for the parish and its vision and mission. If some hard decisions cannot be made, the parish runs the risk of continuing with lackluster mediocrity and maintenance of the status quo.

Here is what we found regarding communication for parishes in Western New York. We are sharing this information here to inform and inspire all parishes to evaluate their communication strategies. Let's begin with the bulletin.

BULLETIN

The parishes with the most outstanding bulletins of those we studied were St. John Vianney Church in Orchard Park, New York; St. Gregory the Great in Williamsville, New York; St. Mary's in Swormville, New York; St. Mary of the Angels Basilica in Olean, New York; and the Church of the Annunciation in Elma, New York.

These parishes had bulletins of six to eight pages, and some had additional inserts up to twelve pages. The parishes did not worry about the cost of printing and the size of the font for ease of reading, so the pages were not jammed with little info boxes. No doubt their communication budgets were ample, too, as evidenced by all the ads. Every bulletin was in color, with updated pictures and current graphics. A church may only wish advertising from parishioners. This prevents advertising dilemmas not in keeping with Christian values.

The bulletins were sectioned by age groups, including a page for youth, one for the elderly, and one for the family. There were sections allotted to ministries and to faith formation. Upcoming events had a standard placement in the bulletin for months in advance so parishioners could plan ahead. Ministries were reported on, always with invitations to join them. Parishioners looking for some way to give back to the church could get to know about the ministries in the bulletin, as well as the organizational chart offering the time, the meeting place, the projects being worked on, and how to reach the ministry leader. This way a busy parishioner could see which ministries fit into their schedules and lives. These bulletins also included bullet points on the weekend message to help parishioners refresh the meaning of the Word of God in living a Christian life.

These bulletins also clearly listed their vision, mission, and motto at the front, under the name of the parish, as well the address and phone number. (It surprised us that the address was not visible on every parish's bulletin. One had the street address but no town. This information matters for viewers looking up bulletins on the website for Mass times and address especially visitors from out of town, or those who are interested in visiting and perhaps learning more about the Catholic Church.)

The bulletin and the website should complement each other. Most parishes we visited sorely lacked this comple-

RESTORING TRUST IN THE CATHOLIC PARISH

mentarity. By reviewing and discussing with others who are doing it well, we can develop better communication by replicating what works in our own parishes.

WEBSITES AND VIDEOS

Websites are vital for a parish. Within minutes of first examination, a parishioner or potential new parishioner will write off attending church or participating with a parish. If the branding of the website does not give the viewer a good impression, feeling or a consistent and wholesome message, and the information sought after, the viewer will leave the site unimpressed and unmotivated. This is where branding comes in. Take a look at a multilevel marketing platform, for instance. They design a quality platform and then roll out quality websites for each distributor. Each distributor can customize their own website but the bones or skeleton is provided by the parent corporation with all the basics about the products, history, trials and news. It is cost efficient and saves time. Furthermore, most parishes do not have the expertise necessary to develop useful and appealing websites. And so, they end up with outdated colors and pictures and graphics. Perhaps we should consider that it is too late in the game to render a facelift to every parish left to its own and to save on time and expenses seek the help from corporate meaning the chancery.

The Diocese of Buffalo chancery website can offer a branding platform for their parishes. However, there needs to be a website council before the facelifts commences. For instance, the diocese website page on the sex abuse scan-

dals has a banner and pop-ups asking for financial donations. There are no words to express on the strategy behind
this branding. The laity must step forward with advice and
direction making up a website council. A website marketing company can create a wholesome platform for the diocese with a website council input.

The website council is a body with goal directed
action. Form follows function. Figure out what you want
the website to accomplish and in what order. The website
needs to have energy, be unified, clear, clean, full of life,
awake and engaging. Illuminate the strengths, critically
think the barriers and obstacles, and reach for opportunities to be welcoming, helpful and inspiring. On both the
diocese website and the parish website the goal is to have
visitors return to the website on a regular basis for fellowship, evangelization and making stronger disciples for the
Lord. In order to accomplish this, the website needs to help
people grow in their spirituality and knowledge of scripture and the Lord. A strong dose of fellowship is the icing
on the cake. For those less inclined to the social, ample
opportunities for prayer, adoration, Mass and scripture
studies are the key including virtual. Many parishes cannot provide these but can connect the website viewer with
YouTube videos, music, books, essays, Catholic TV stations, publishers and societies, etc. Once the discipleship
and evangelization begins to grow, ministries will develop
exponentially. Perhaps, now is a good time to encourage
the Bishop to speak to his flock on a monthly basis by both
video and by letter in the bulletin. During crisis, the peo-

ple need his presence especially with answers forthcoming. Silence is the worst for revitalizing the parishes.

The parishes we visited that had the best websites were St. John Vianney Church in Orchard Park, New York; St. Gregory the Great in Williamsville, New York; St. Mary's in Swormville, New York; and St. Mary of the Angels Basilica in Olean, New York.

Outside of our diocese, we found two outstanding websites: St. Matthew's in Charlotte, North Carolina, and St. Joseph Bread of Life in Erie, Pennsylvania.

St. Matthew's uses social media to share parishioner testimonies and how they pursue deepening their faith walk. The parish videotaped studies focused on the Bible, the Cardinal Virtues, and the Commandments. These videos may be viewed by parishioners so they can watch from home and nursing homes without even doing the readings, yet benefiting and growing from the input of the participants. Talk about getting the most out of studies! These videos can be viewed from a cell phone, tablet, or computer.

St. Matthew's has its own media crew and equipment, so their videos are very good quality. They cover privacy concerns and have the support of parishioners. The filmed parish activities became evidence-based films indicating a thriving, enthusiastic, and spiritually on-fire faith community of all age groups.

The website for St. Joseph Bread of Life presents a wonderful welcome and invitation from pastor Fr. Larry

Richards. All of his homilies and sermons are available on the website; his humor and down-to-earth examples of how to live the faith each day and apply the Scripture readings are very relevant. He seems to speak directly to people on an intimate level, and this is the beauty of his approach.

Typically, people go to church websites for Mass times and location when they do not have a bulletin, or when they are visiting from out of town or from another parish. Parishioners seldom visit their parish's website unless they have a particular need and the parish office is closed.

A parish website should be the sort of place parishioners want to visit often. A website should draw people to catch up on parish activities and news about parishioners. It should be a place for spiritual direction, inspiring videos, book reviews and recommendations, and music. These are seriously lacking in most parish websites.

The website is also a place to feature ministries. A website is an opportunity to tell what a ministry does, who makes up the ministry, the current projects, place of meeting, when they meet, and who can provide more information about it. The website can invite people to join the ministry. It would be helpful to list some of the skills and talents needed. (This was seldom evidenced on the websites of parishes we visited.)

A website can also be a place to rebuild trust. In general, parishioners are accosted for money by their parishes, but they don't see what value their parish is bringing to their life. We need to rebuild trust, and this begins by showing

restoration and signs of life in the Church rather than asking for money. Although access to online donations is easy for some, this should not be the goal of the parish website. Emphasize spiritual growth and fellowship, not money. Fundraising gets old and smacks of consumerism, not spiritual growth. The objective is to aid all interested in finding a way to further explore and develop their faith. A goal should be to find and share the joy in becoming a joy-filled community that financially supports its parish.

A tech-savvy website can appeal to kids and to young adults. These groups are often lost to our parishes and could be brought back into the fold if we offered topics interesting to them with studies and prayer. The parish website could be a place to connect young people and their families, inviting them to join small groups. They can click through the pages to learn what intrigues them. Make topics available to be explored further in small discussion groups; lead them to small groups to explore their faith further. Small groups draw a large parish together by developing a sense of belonging. A tech savvy website can draw families into family Bible studies and prayer, especially when linked to other families in a small group.

A parish website should be the family go-to for questions about the Catechism, lives of the saints, the Commandments, and other topics of interest. These might include Christian child-rearing, budgeting, and being a good steward of what God has given, making friends, sharing the gospel, and inviting people to church.

A website is an opportunity for the priests to help laity apply weekly readings to everyday life. A website can offer chat options on controversial Catholic topics discussed in the Catholic Register or on EWTN.

The parish website can provide connecting with the sick (those sick who wish to be contacted) to encourage them by offering a link to an E-card website enabling an easy way to send get well and congratulations cards. Parishioners can ask if a visit to the sick or a nursing home resident is welcomed.

People love to watch videos, especially funny or engaging ones. Parish websites should post videos of live streamed Masses, the parish Rosary, the Stations of the Cross, or parish council meetings. In fact, every month a member can share their video testimony of faith. This can draw parishioners to the website regularly. These videos can be about the living or a deceased loved one, or juxtaposing current events in society and showing how the parish can respond as Christ would. One of the complaints of fallen-away Catholics is that Sunday messages are not relevant to real life. The website provides an opportunity to make it relevant.

The website is an opportunity to involve, include, and grow membership so that people can more easily give back to God and to the Church.

Websites are not a fad or optional for Catholic parishes. They are critical for reaching parishioners today, especially our youth, millennials, and young families. A good website can be instrumental in drawing Catholics back, and satisfying and feeding the flock. Spiritual growth depends on it, because once-a-week church attendance is not enough to maintain the faith of the flock. The website is an opportunity to use an engaging, interactive tool to inspire parishioners to join ministry studies, read blogs, attend meetings, foster charitable works of mercy, and grow in faith and fellowship in order to develop and maintain growth in a parish.

There are a vast number of YouTube videos on all sorts of Catholic topics that a website can guide the flock to access. Books and videos are plentiful as well. Firstly, there needs to be a council set up with parish staff and tech smart laity. They need to research policies established in churches without having to reinvent the wheel. Policies have already been written, if not by one diocese, then by another archdiocese. Scot Landry shows how to create digital ministries and become digital missionaries in the Catholic Church through website development. His book *Transforming Parish Communications* (Our Sunday Visitor, 2014) delivers practical and straightforward tips. Policies will cover legal considerations, safety, security, and code of conduct. The council or committee will decide on a schedule and timeline to launch over a one-year period. It begins with a campaign from the pulpit to submit email addresses. (Children under eighteen may submit email addresses only through parents.)

Every ministry and society needs a page on the website with mandatory monthly updates. The pastor or pastoral administrator or parish life coordinator will be able to see if there is enough growth or if the ministry needs attention. The website is the greatest beacon to share and reach out to new members. It shows the life of the parish. Videos and podcasts should be evident on every ministry site. This way spiritual growth is shared and an opportunity to see the ministry in action. In fact, every month a member can be sharing their videoed testimony of faith. This can draw the parish to the website regularly. It can be about the living or a deceased loved one. As the Lord spoke in parables, juxtapose it to a current event in society and show how the parish can respond as Christ would. One of the complaints of fallen away Catholics is that Sunday messages are not relevant to real life. Here is an opportunity to make it relevant in the website. This is why we are Catholic and here is how to live the gospel in real action.

EMAIL AND SOCIAL MEDIA

Emails are another valuable means of communication, giving parishioners the plan of action and description of the bulletins and websites. Emails can invite to join a blog on a faith topic, or a new development in the parish. It can invite to answer a survey if parish life, or parish council, or the priest has a query of the parishioners.

Many churches are using the Flocknote program to communicate with parishioners, staff and other churches. It is affordable because cost is based on volume as the church grows. Breeze is another alternative for church emails, messaging and texts. There is a variety of software for all aspects of church management including finances, minutes, projects, ministries, etc.

If the parish priest already writes to the parishioners in the bulletin on a subject of his interest or related to the weekly readings, this can be turned into a blog so that parishioners may ask questions subsequently for input. Blogs can be written on countless subjects that parishioners grapple with in life.

Social media is also a great way to reach parishioners. Consider using Facebook and Twitter and Instagram, as long as it is not personal Facebook pages. The objective is to foster fellowship and Catholic community. One of the greatest ways to build community and pique the interest of those shopping for a church is using videotaped interactions at the parish. It is much more convincing than pictures in this technological age. Recorded videos of parish picnics, banquets, fish fries, school projects, and outreach projects show how much life is in the parish. Those seeking a church home can easily size up the life of a parish this way and determine whether they want to belong.

PARISH LIFE HANDBOOK

A parish life handbook is a vital means to connect parishioners and potential members by showing the life blood of the parish. St. Gregory the Great Parish, Buffalo, New York, and St. Matthew's Church of Charlotte, North Carolina, did this in their handbooks. All ministries are listed with leader names, contact info, purpose of the group, meeting place and times, as well as projects. The handbook is a comprehensive tool for any volunteer to plan a schedule with work and home life. It is one of the very best market-ing tools as a secondary benefit.

TECHNOLOGY AND SOUND

Big screen TVs in the nave of the church are common in progressive and growing Catholic churches. St. Joseph Bread of Life had them on both sides of the cathedral-like church. Hymns and readings were displayed by a designated IT person during the Masses. It made following the Mass easy for non-Catholics visiting and for converts. It enabled sight-challenged people to read and to sing with ease.

Father Larry Richards would beckon for all to sing loudly and from the heart. A resounding response came after a few times of his encouraging, "You can do better." It created enthusiasm and joy. One could feel the Spirit moving. The best example in western New York was at St. Leo the Great. It incorporated musical instruments as well, like string instruments.

At the Church of the Annunciation in Elma, New York, the acoustics were excellent (in part due to the ceiling design), one could hear oneself sing loudly. It was extraordinary how it improved one's own voice.

For some parishes, the feedback from the speaker system, particularly at the front of the nave, created reverberation which caused hardship for the elderly with hearing aids. It is surprising that even when parishioners voiced a complaint, the parish was slow to act on it. This is where communication comes in. If parishioners feel the church does not care, they will leave. At the very least, send them an email.

Father Binoy Davis at St. Matthew's Church emphasizes the critical need to start Utube, Instagram, Facebook and WeChat pages for all parishes to reach out to all age groups. With as many as 40,000 parishioners at his parish, it is the best way to keep Catholics in touch.

Don't under estimate the value of the Big Welcome from the pulpit, at the door and by parishioners after Mass. Extending out a handshake and introducing oneself goes a long way to cheer new-comers; After a while faces and names are recognized and a sense of belonging develops.

> *Oh Lord, teach us to serve out of love for You as You served out of love for us and for the Father.*

CHAPTER 4

STRATEGY FOR ORGANIZATION

THE ORGANIZATIONAL CHART

Most parishioners cannot say how many ministries are available in their parish. Most do not know what each ministry actually does or who belongs or leads them. It is no wonder, then, that ministries are not growing. This is why an organizational contact chart is vital. St. John Vianney of Orchard Park, New York, has done this very well, headed by the Parish Life Committee, which has since been absorbed by a new parish council. In some parishes a stewardship committee is organized to oversee ministries.

The organizational chart is brilliant because it enables everyone to see all the information required by a parishioner to make decisions. This organizational chart should become the standard for all parishes, even for small ones. For readers who are interested in learning how this can be structured, I have included the organizational chart for St. John Vianney, Orchard Park, New York, in an appendix to this book.

Each ministry should have its spotlight moment each year, beginning from the pulpit, and elaborated on in the bulletin and on the website.

VIDEO EACH MINISTRY

A five minute video of all the ministries should be created and played at the coffee and donut hour after Mass. People should be able to view it in the narthex (foyer) of the church and at all gatherings. Not only is it of interest because it features parishioners, but it builds identity and community. It may easily encourage new members to join the parish. Remember, people looking for a new parish want to see how much life there is in the parish to make a decision on whether to join.

EXAMPLES OF HEALTHY MINISTRIES

ST. JOSEPH'S WORKSHOP

One of the best organized ministries we saw was at the Church of the Annunciation in Elma, New York. A group of twelve retired men skilled in plumbing, electric, and carpentry formed St Joseph's Workshop. They took over the basement of the original church building, which was no longer used for Masses as the church had been replaced by a larger, more modern one on the same campus.

This group was very organized and committed five days of the week to the ministry. They donated all their tools from home. Their work produced tens of thousands of dollars in repair and maintenance, free of charge for the parish. They made furniture for the youth group stationed on the main floor of the old church, which was just above the workshop. The St. Joseph's Workshop made tables and chairs for the youth Bible study, fellowship, and for dining. They built a refreshment snack bar for them, too, and added games. Another enterprise by this ministry included building birdhouses, swings, and lawn chairs for the annual auction fundraiser. They also built furniture for needy families identified through the St. Vincent DePaul Society.

The St. Joseph's Workshop ministry began their day with coffee and breakfast. These men also took turns cooking a hot lunch for the group eating at their self-made long dining table and chairs. They added Bible study and prayer in between. They worked for free in their amazing, well-stocked and equipped workshop. The day ended with beer and snacks. The shop, by the way, was furnished with their own exceptional tools and materials such as wire, tons of bolts and screws, nails, and pvc pipe, which they had organized very carefully in their stock room.

THE SEWING BEES

The women of this parish had organized a sewing-bee, making dresses for poor women in Haiti. This ministry too was well organized. The dresses were simply designed, with cheery colors to communicate to the women recipients that they were treasured and mattered. The dresses were made on kind of an assembly line. Some of the women traced the patterns, some cut the pattern, some went to the cupboard and took a package for sewing at home. Others would press and package the finished dresses for shipping to Haiti. Naturally, there was good fellowship and prayer in this ministry, and they were proud of it.

MEALS FOR THE HUNGRY

At St. Matthew's in Charlotte, North Carolina, whole families would gather in the auditorium to put together meals, and package them for the hungry poor in Charlotte. For the children this activity would count for religious education requirements. The essential aspect of this ministry was that it was done as a family. Families will always have this memory of service together.

EUCHARISTIC MINISTERS

St. Matthew's had a unique set-up where three, sometimes four, Eucharistic ministers would show up at each Mass, including all three daily Masses Monday through Friday, to take the Holy Eucharist to the homebound and to the sick.

St. Matthew's is a parish of over 35,000 people, so naturally they have to be exceptionally well organized to maintain 110 to 140 ministries at the same church. They somehow are combining spiritual growth into the ministries, going beyond just doing and serving. This is done with prayer, scriptural reflections, and faith sharing.

WELCOME MINISTRY

The welcome ministry offered a comprehensive, beautiful newcomer's folder with everything a newcomer needs to know. Each newcomer was greeted personally and shown what the folder contained. Questions were answered. People were greeted by an enthusiastic welcome minister. However, when the welcome minister was not available or needed help, parishioners stepped in and assisted the newcomers to become informed. These parishioners were ready to talk about the parish. (If a parish is able to include parishioners in their marketing education, it can be a very successful policy for bringing in newcomers or Catholics who wish to return.) Their enthusiasm for their parish was contagious. Once completed, the registration form was deposited into the box at the welcome station. The registration included the parish commitment between pastor and prospective parishioner, and it was signed by both. This inquiry was followed up promptly within a couple of days and enthusiastically with the information requested. This is part of the reason St. Matthew's has grown. The love for the parish was clearly evidenced by the enthusiastic flock.

NURSERY MINISTRY

There are three common complaints about Catholic parishes voiced by young families today, and actually they are the same that have been shared for many decades, but ignored. (Thus, young families go elsewhere, often to Evangelical churches, because they offer fun and productive solutions, and they do it so well.)

The first of the common complaints is how to ignore crying babies and bored toddlers, plus jittery preschoolers and playful, sometimes rambunctious elementary schoolers. What is the best way to solve this problem?

St. Matthew's offered two options. They had a very beautifully designed nursery for children of different ages up to five years. They also had a program for the children so children enjoyed staying, making new friends. Nursery networked with other ministries during the week to encourage attendance by taking care of their children. Babysitters were available to come to the home should parents prefer this avenue. Adults and teenagers offered their time as a ministry.

Here is a nice (funny) story from St. Matthew's about their nursery ministry.

....

A small child in the church nursery was drawing a picture and the nursery attendant came up to her and asked what she was drawing. The child remarked she was drawing a picture of God. The attendant sweetly remarked, "Well you know no one has seen God and knows what He looks like." The child retorted, "Give me a minute to finish and I will show you what He looks like."

....

LIVING YOUR STRENGTHS

St. Matthew's offers a very helpful program called **Living Your Strengths** to develop ministries. The program is on their church website. Once parishioners discover their strengths, they join a small group of ten people for several weeks for ninety minutes per week to explore opportunities. Living Your Strengths is based on the Gallup's Clifton StrengthsFinder®, an online assessment tool. This program is organized several times per year and can be a virtual class also. St. Matthew's has developed its own version, which they make available to other parishes. It requires two coaches and two facilitators. They make a point of emphasizing that it is not a recruitment tool for ministries but to build up parishioners to know their purpose in life and their gifts from God.

Here are several ministries unique to restoring trust in the Catholic Parish by meeting the needs of parishioners and as taken from the parish handbook.

CHRIST RENEWS HIS PARISH

This is a unique, parish-based faith renewal experience for men and women. This parishioner-led experience is designed to foster a sense of community within the parish. Participants will grow in discipleship and come away with renewed spirit and strengthened faith.

DISCIPLESHIP GROUPS FOR HIGH SCHOOL YOUTH MINISTRY

Following the small group model, teens come together to further their knowledge of the Faith, deepen their relationship with Christ, and grow in community with each other. Groups are gender specific, and adults are needed to help facilitate group lessons and discussions.

MOMS GROUP

Moms Group supports the vocation of motherhood by strengthening faith through various books and studies applicable to Catholic family life. Mothers of all ages and stages are invited to join. They meet one morning each week throughout the school year with the benefit of childcare provided through the church nursery.

WELCOME HOME FOR RETURNING CATHOLICS

This program offers a one-on-one companion to walk with the returning individual as they journey the path to full communion with the Body of Christ. Companions will listen, encourage and suggest Church resources and programs to foster growth in both sacramental and spiritual life, particularly the sacraments of reconciliation and Eucharist. There are no structured classes, but interactions tailored to individual needs and schedules.

FAMILY CONNECTIONS

This ministry hosts a variety of engaging and joyful events for the whole family that makes faith fun. The purpose is to unite the family and also unite with the family of the parish.

NEWCOMERS GROUP

A nine-week discussion group for ladies new to the parish, based on the book *After Boxes are Unpacked: Moving On After Moving In.*

SENIORS THAT ARE RETIRED (STARS)

Program provides fellowship for older adults. Activities include monthly meetings with lunch, programs, and entertainment; as well as day and overnight bus trips.

SUNDAY PRESCHOOL TO KINDERGARDEN

Offered on Sunday mornings during the morning Masses, high school teen and adult catechists shepherd the children through crafts, stories, prayers and activities based on the Sunday Gospel.

UNBOUND

The program offers sessions that guide the individual adult to healing and restoration from past and present spiritual and emotional hurts. The model provides insight into what might be blocking an individual's ability to experience freedom in Christ, allowing healing and restoration through the power of the Holy Spirit.

NETWORKING FOR GROWTH

Write out a new mission and vision for the ministry that meets the needs of fellow Catholics and those not coming to church any longer. Re-invest in the society by reinventing it. Dead wood is only good for burning. Let the Lord bring new life. Where there is life there is the Holy Spirit. As Catholics, we recite and believe in the Apostles Creed when we say, "I believe in the Holy Spirit, the Lord, the giver of life."

There are many needs in the parish and in the community. Helping in the nursery may lead to ministry to a family where grandparents live far away. Some voids may be filled by modeling a loving grandparent. Assisting with youth group functions is a way adult ministries can model care and interest in the younger folk. These are examples of how a ministry can integrate into other ministries and into the entire parish.

A strong policy on gossip makes for a strong organization. Leave no allowance for gossip. Shut it down right away with a set policy.

Have a policy, when one member suffers, all gather around in prayer to comfort and heal. Create a policy that keeps what is said and shared in the group with the group. Be faithful to the brothers and sisters in Christ, thus honoring the Lord and what He has done in each and every person.

Come Holy Spirit and enkindle in us the fires of your love.

CHAPTER 5

REVITALIZATION PROGRAMS

PARISH ASSESSMENT

This chapter begins on a somber note. Apologies given, but there are some realities we have to face as the Catholic Church in Western New York, Diocese of Buffalo.

In assessing elements of a parish, Kathleen and I considered 165 elements from altar decorations to the effectiveness of the homily, to the participation of the congregation, ministries, bulletin, and website, etc. We gave parishes a rating for each element on a scale of 1 to 5. The total for the parish was converted to a scale of 1 to 10.

Without question each parish has the potential to rate much higher given the proper tools and assistance, which are lacking in the current system. Sadly, most of the parishes in Western New York totaled **3.5 out of 10**. There is so much potential, but these churches exist without much life.

Some of the Catholic parishes we ranked function at a **1 or 2 out of 10**. They are in critical care mode, and each one is alive only due to the service of a few people in their parishes who multi-task or wear many hats, from cleaning the church, to sacristan, to bringing Communion to the sick, and sometimes music ministry. These parishes are desperately in need of a lifeline. Many are in rural areas, while others are in small urban centers where there are multiple Catholic parishes. The future of these ailing parishes, in all likelihood, will be that they will close, requiring some parishioners to travel up to thirty minutes for Mass.

We found there were Catholic parishes in the Diocese of Buffalo, New York, that we would rank as 8s, which could become 10s. There were too few of them. These outstanding Catholic parishes could teach us and help lead us, and, in the process, help their own parishes to become 10s.

RANKINGS OF PARISHES

- 1-2 CRITICAL STATE

- 3-4 ACUTE CARE

- 5-6 SIGNS OF RECOVERY & HEALTH

- 7-8 MANAGING, STRONG VITALS

- 9-10 EXCEPTIONAL

Our objective on this journey of faith is to study each church we visited with the same approach: we observed, analyzed, then reported on outstanding features, as well as areas we believe need improvement. We seek to be impartial, but positive. Let's consider the following model of a parish that was failing and is now prospering. Perhaps using our case study of St. Philomena Parish in Franklinville, New York, will better illustrate what we mean. We were especially interested in St. Philomena because others had called it an example of "what the twenty-first-century Catholic Church should resemble." We learned that St. Philomena was remarkable in the Diocese of Buffalo for having gone from insolvency to solvency in just over two years.

After the passing of their pastor in early 2017, with only 150 families on the parish roster, Deacon Richard Matthews took the helm, and Rev. Christopher Okali, provided the Sacraments. Lay people took on leadership roles. Approximately one and a half years later, Fr. Okali was reassigned, and Deacon Matthews was joined by the new regional Pastor Rev. F. Patrick Melfi, and regional parochial vicars Rev. David Tourville and Rev. Romulo Montero of Olean, New York. At this point St. Philomena became linked to the new tri-parish of Southern Tier Catholic Community. All of this led to the accomplishment of their miracle.

The motto at St. Philomena parish has been "Everything happens for a reason and everyone is responsible for what happens." The lay people, along with their financial and parish councils, became accountable for the daily administration of the parish, allowing the clergy team of the parish to do what they were trained to do: act as the spiritual and sacramental leaders.

Believing that faith formation was intended and needed by the entire parish, the team of clergy and laity coordinated faith formation instruction with age-appropriate activities for adults, young adults, and children of every age. Everyone had "homework" based on the themes each month, the Sacraments, lives of the saints, Church history, and the Liturgy. It cannot be over-emphasized that each parishioner took ownership for learning "assignments," which were written, drawn, acted out, sung, or centered on a family activity. As a result, spiritual growth of adults and their families was connected to the parish as a whole.

Originally as a cost-saving measure, the parish implemented the use of technology during the Liturgy, with installed television screens and a wireless link to a computer. This way PowerPoints could be used to focus the community worship with those parishioners around them rather than from a missal or hymnal. Therefore, the true focus could be on the Liturgy of the Word and Eucharist. Worship with technology tied the parish together in one strong voice during Mass.

Implementing technology has led to positive outcomes during the current Covid-19 pandemic, with live-streamed Masses and liturgical services celebrated by the clergy team, again strengthening the connection between the Church and her people.

St. Philomena Parish participated in family Rosaries, Reconciliation services, and social gatherings to bring both the nuclear family and the bigger parish family together, all of which strengthened communication and faith-bonds. From there, more ministries grew. This was the ideal progression of a parish. Individual spiritual growth expanded to reaching out to others, and to corporal works of mercy.

One of the larger fundraisers this parish participated in was the Philomena Fest, which celebrated their patroness on the second Sunday of August. Each year the entire parish participated, taking part in the Mass and procession that led to their parish fete for the day. The charitable spirit of the congregation was reflected in their giving not only of their treasure to the weekly collection, but also to support the local Catholic Charities food pantry and other community causes.

The web and Facebook pages for St. Philomena are informative, with schedules for Masses and Sacraments as well as links to both sister parishes, the diocese, and the larger Catholic Church around the world.

The vibrancy of this parish today is owing to the collaboration and symbiosis between forward-thinking clerics and committed lay people. St. Philomena is an example of how collaboration can work, even with a limited number of families in the parish. Appreciation is extended to Janet Vant for her contribution of the story.

Contributed by Kathleen McGough Johnson

We have some ideas for other parishes that want to move from surviving to thriving, as St. Philomena Parish did. This movement will require a paradigm shift. Here are some suggestions:

A.   Utilize a consultant group comprised of several experts to work with individual parish laity.

B.   Share our analysis of the church with the parish council in person.

C.   Analyze and present an example of a successful model and the steps to take to be successful.

STIMULUS BEGINNING WITH THE CHANCERY

1.   Propose a stimulus package to launch a restoration program RP for youth and adults for spiritual development and fellowship with the goal in mind to further the mission of discipleship and evangelization. The restoration grant would pay for a youth minister who would be shared by up to three churches in a small urban area or for a parish with a minimum of 4,000 parishioners.

2.   Propose a stop-gap proposal of emergency services for parishes experiencing acute distress syndrome (ADS). The parishes in the acute distress syndrome program would not pay any percentage of parish collection and donations to the diocese or to the archdiocese for a period

of two years, giving them time to restructure and revive the parish.

3.   The **ADS grant** would pay for consultation services and programs up to $50,000 for two years. If success is not achieved by membership and donation of time, talent and treasure, the proposal would include closing the parish. This gives the parish community a heads-up and time to respond. Consultants specializing in parish revitalization would become immediately involved upon the acute distress syndrome alert. ADS program notification progress reports would be expected on a quarterly basis.

4.   Celebrate the revitalization program (RP) wins for each parish. This could be done through bulletins and websites throughout the diocese. There needs to be a change in attitude regarding care and brotherly love towards other parishes, whether they are prospering or not. We need this rather than a cold shoulder coming from a competitive culture in a parish.

5.   Propose a grant for IT (Internet Technology) called ITRP. Its purpose would be to rebuild and modernize the technology in the church during Masses and on the website. The grant would be available for two years, providing time to get the work done. The same IT person would be available for up to three parishes. The grant would include monies for an educated IT per-

son trained in parish communication and not currently on staff at the parish. It would pay for two new computers, four 65-inch screens, and a media computer with iogear to connect all the screens for church Masses in the main church (additional speakers as needed). The IT person would be shared to set up the broadcasts and be available to reconstruct the websites for up to three parishes.

The revitalization grants would be for those parishes ranking between 1 and 4 only. Those parishes are showing signs of acute distress. If there is money to spare than welcome parishes in the 5-6 ranking which are those showing signs of recovery and health. The program would catapult them into the next category of managing, strong vitals.

The grants would be upward of $100,000 each, and parishes would be able to apply for both the RP and the ITRP for two consecutive years. We propose funding would come from the diocese or from private donors, or from Upon This Rock fund campaign. Perhaps consider the grant as a reconciliation gift from the chancery?

Thank you, Lord, for your servants, the laity of the parish, the givers of time, talent and treasure.

CHAPTER 6

REGIONALIZATION

"Every church parish has room to grow." This is what Father Darrell Duffy of St. James Church in Jamestown, New York, says. As we reviewed in previous chapters, we found this to be true in our research for both communication and organization in parishes. The goal is to increase time, talent, and treasure for each member of the parish in some way.

After understanding regionalism, its usefulness in the church can be shown with examples of how it can bolster ministries.

Regionalism in the Church is not for political reasons, administrative, cultural, religious, geography, or for linguistic reasons. Regionalism is regarding an area such as western New York state diocese of Buffalo for the sole purpose of networking for spiritual revival, sharing information, wisdom, and resources, and relationship-building with others doing the same function. A ministry in a parish is still independent but relies on help from other locations in an interdependent way. It can be done on a smaller scale such as by city or county.

REVIVING MINISTRIES

The regionalization model can be assigned to struggling ministries. As parishes age, there are fewer members in Altar and Rosary Societies, Catholic Daughter Society, Knights of Columbus, and St. Vincent DePaul Society. An organized regional group has a better chance for new energy, a vibrant program, and growth. The individual parish societies can still meet at their own parishes as well, but when a group like Altar and Rosary Society has stopped praying the Rosary together and has minimal responsibility for the sacristy, but to donate some money for linens and change the candles, then infusion of creative ideas and energy is warranted. When no one wants to join the groups even after several failed membership drives, it is time for availability of regional leadership to develop the ministries. The ministries that succeed are those that have a spiritual development program. From there, prayer ensues and creativity develops with corporal works of mercy to follow.

Groups such as Altar and Rosary Societies provide a stash or reservoir of faith and love, from which the entire parish can benefit. This reservoir is for the most part untapped, however. Think about all of the groups on whom these societies can have an impact: the youth, the addicted groups, the unwed mothers, the shut-ins, those who are all alone, etc. There is endless opportunity to witness, to encourage, sharing what God is doing in their lives, creating hope.

These role models may be essentially dormant, and this is why church societies are not alive. Some serve a purpose by doing corporal works of mercy, but if they would share the joy of the Lord, the membership would increase. The song taught to little ones, "This little light of mine, I'm going to let it shine" is the hope to others. It is the challenge to current members. Find ways to let it shine. Use music, which is a double prayer from one heart with all hearts to sing the praises of the Lord. Voices may be embellished with instruments if there is doubt about good voices. Show the life of Christ from your souls. Let it shine.

Revisit the ministry or society vision and mission statement with a new mission and vision that meets the needs of fellow Catholics and those not coming to church any longer.

YOUTH GROUP

Regionalization can work for a youth group. If two parishes want a youth group, but one has an ideal location while another has more of other necessities, a combined effort creating one regional youth group may be the solution.

Resources to establish a youth group may come from both parishes to create a combined ownership. This way, time, talent, and treasure flows from multiple directions.

Consequently, the youth feel free to attend regardless of parish affiliation. This may further extend into a regional confirmation class, not just a regional confirmation ceremony. The group may become large enough to designate a youth group center or building on the campus of one of the parishes. A youth group by region of a rural area, or small urban center results in more youth group resources. This will create a strong, diverse program and increase membership.

A Youth Mass can travel to individual parishes by season of the year or simply remain at one designated Mass each Sunday. Five o'clock p.m. seems to be the best time to ensure attendance. This seemed to be the most popular with other churches that experimented with youth schedules. This time allows the youth to finish Mass and be present at family Sunday dinners for those that have to get back home. Priests and deacons could be invited from all parishes nearby. Youth Mass should be open to all parishioners on a Sunday evening.

Some parishes may not favor sharing a youth group, but there is so much effort to make the program successful, fun, and solid for the spiritual growth of youth and development of Catholic character that it can become daunting. Sharing youth groups avoids exhaustion for individual parishes that need to seek out the right time, talent, and resources to run a youth group.

When youth ministry is done successfully, membership pours in because the program is dynamic and exciting. The youth invite friends from many places. Parents are happy when the kids are happy and thriving in their faith. Great examples are Saint Gregory the Great Church in Buffalo, New York, and St. Matthew's church in Charlotte, North Carolina.

A grant of $100,000 plus (from the RP Revitalization Program recommended in chapter 5) could cover two permanent staff for youth, one male and one female, for a two-year period. The youth pastors may be able to cover youth groups for middle school and for high school. Perhaps the chancery and the diocese could assist monetarily with this effort for two years until proof of a successful youth group is established. Thereafter, the parishes can take over the costs. Parishioner patrons may be inspired to come forward with support when the program ROI is determined with sufficient proof of testimonies.

Regionalization takes the nuggets of gold, the gems of faith that exist in each parish, and then shares and builds on those strengths. This sharing is needed for spiritual growth. From there come the corporal works of mercy, which put our faith in action. This becomes part of the parish ROI (return on investment). The joy and light of Christ shines. And the pastor is amazed because all the work is getting done and all of it is important. Father Tim Koester, pastor of Precious Blood Church, Angola, New York, sings the praises of his flock. Their motto, "Doing little things with great love," is clearly reflected on a day-by-day basis. Although a tiny parish, the light is shining brightly in this parish.

It is very difficult for one or two priests to accomplish everything. The main jobs of a parish priest are to administer the Sacraments and give the homily. The flock has great hunger, yet too often the flock is maintained on a diet that keeps the appetite down. How often have we heard messages made of pablum? Can we assume that the flock is ready for messages with real meat? How often have we heard it said the message was forgotten before leaving the church building?

Yet if we consider that all ministries are responsible for the discipleship and evangelization of others, we have a different view of what it means to be parish. The motto of St. Philomena Parish rings true here: "Everything happens for a reason and everyone is responsible for what happens." The point is not to undermine the priest, but to assist in the mission and the vision of the parish, to proclaim the Good News and bring in the herd.

How does a group of parishes begin a regional approach? There are several steps, to be found in the next section.

REGIONAL PROGRAM

Some priests may say they use the "clustering" approach, which refers to priests being responsible for more than one parish. Regionalization is different in that it touches more on the laity building the shared programs together. Regionalization also includes the priest attempting to meet the needs of more than one parish.

To begin, hold a regional meeting or convention by invitation to all locations for one particular group, society, or ministry. Request everyone to pray the Rosary before coming to the regional conference. Have a meet-and-greet with food and coffee beforehand. Present two 20-minute speakers to introduce the situation or the Why we are here (the objective of the meeting).

Conduct a brainstorming session of bright and best ideas. Brainstorm mission and vision for a regional group. Assign posts for the regional board by volunteers willing to give one year of time and commitment. Leadership must have computer, email, and communication skills.

Break out into local parish groups. Spend a one-hour session on the mission and the vision for the parish group. Share with the regional group or the group at large. Break out for a meal. (These one-hour sessions with local groups can also be held at the individual parishes prior to the regional meeting.)

For the afternoon session, choose one project that reflects the mission and vision for the parish group. By combining parishes, parishes describe the management of the project and the anticipated outcome. Begin each section of the program with prayer. There is no room for competition, jealousy, or exclusivity. The goal is to create welcoming, a show of assistance, and a sense of belonging to the ministry with the purpose of fulfilling God's call for the ministry itself.

The Regional board, comprised of priest, deacon or parish administrator, members of board of Trustees, Parish Council, and Parish Life, of all parishes should send a summary of the conference to each parish. Within thirty-days of the conference, each parish or group of parishes formed must send in reports to the regional board on the progress made. The time frame would be set by the regional board, perhaps for a quarterly basis. Zoom meetings can be used regularly.

This type of regional exercise can re-invent and re-energize the ministries and societies. It is vital for the longevity, health, and wellbeing of the parish groups. The other role of the board is to maintain contact with each parish group, share resources, and answer questions on an as-needed basis. The regionalization of the group in the diocese can become an annual event featuring the outcomes, the successes, and the wins for failing ministries. A blog can keep the groups together while learning from the regional board throughout the year.

REGIONAL PROGRAM BECOMES FAMILY OF PARISHES

The regional program in planning terms has become referred to as the Family of Parishes in the Diocese of Buffalo in late 2020. It is the same concept but in the Diocese of Buffalo it begins with a pilot program which is preceded by the Bishop and Renewal Director leading the way by meeting with each Vicariate. There the concept is introduced and immediate feedback is provided by the priests. The difference between regionalism and the Family of Parishes is that one pastor is designated for several parishes and supported by parochial vicars, deacons and laity from each parish. In order for this to work, the Diocese must provide spiritual direction, leadership training, communication training including internet, workshops on how to work with laity, and project management. Roles for each player must be clearly defined.

The Family of Parishes takes regionalization further than just ministry development. It places one pastor over four to eight catholic churches assisted by parochial vicars, deacons and laity. It involves every aspect of church life. The reason for creation of this model is due to the upheavals the scandals created resulting in a forecast for priest availability up to the year 2030 guesstimated to be 100 which is down from the current 145. This number of priests cannot service the current church total for the diocese of 160 churches. So the model must change in order to avoid church closings. The troubles this may cause must also be mitigated with priest retreats that address and retrain because it is not a model priests were trained with in the seminary. In fact, the goal of priesthood is most often to become a pastor. So be kind to your priests because they are dealing with major change coming down the pike and much more work!

> *You know Lord, what we really need to build up our parishes. Help us to hear the Holy Spirit and help us with the discipline to respond.*

CHAPTER 7

RESTORING TRUST

CLEANING HOUSE

There are many things that have to be done in order to restore trust in the Catholic parish. As a church body of Christ, we recognize many examples of failures by the hierarchy concerning management of ministries, education or catechesis of adults and children, handling of predator priests and the cover-up, management of resources, lack of accountability and transparency, and so on many given in the listening sessions.

The grief and distrust is very real. Compliance measures are a step in the right direction but the silence that accompanies furthers distrust. Let us look at what progress we have made to fix all of the problems.

In 2019, in our parish listening sessions, we witnessed parishioners weeping before the bishop, begging him not to place questionable priests in their parishes while they were being investigated for allegations of sexual abuse. We observed that there is a strict code for child protection in the Catholic Church, with courses and online testing and background checks for the laity, as well. Virtus is a proactive online program to screen and test volunteers and staff who work with children in the Buffalo diocese. It was created by the National Catholic Risk Retention Group in the U.S. and is prodigiously adhered to by all Catholic parishes in the diocese of Buffalo since 2002. As a result of these required training programs and strict protection measures, child abuse cases have been reduced by almost 100 percent in the Diocese of Buffalo. Recognizing this fact, helps to restore trust.

The chancery does due diligence when it receives a report of a priest perpetrating child or older individual abuse, sometimes placing the priest on administrative leave. In confirmed cases in the past, the priest would be sent for rehabilitation to Toronto, Ontario or Philadelphia, PA. This was true for priests sent for rehabilitation from the Diocese of Buffalo. Thereafter, with confirmed reports that the priest was rehabilitated, the priest would be placed in a new location to recommence his ministry. Following decades of this practice, it was discovered that rehab seldom changed the behavior of the individual priest—and this was certainly true for the Diocese of Buffalo. It was a costly lesson for all dioceses. When the Bishop removes a predator priest from serving anywhere it sends a message to the parishioners trust can be restored.

On a parish level, many priests have not adequately addressed the news reports of child abuse with the parishioners. The parishioners sit silently in the pews with many thoughts and questions and emotions. Most parishioners admire their parish priest. They share with their priest through Confession, pray with him, and go through many of life's experiences with him. So when our priests are silent on this subject, parishioners do not know if their priest cares about it or if he is part of the cover-up, or just being a "company man." Even if a priest does offer healing Masses and adds the abused to the Mass prayers of petition, it seems insufficient. It is a beginning, but there needs to be more to help parishioners deal with the grief, brokenness, and anger. We heard plenty of these sentiments in the MRT (Movement to Restore Trust) parish listening sessions.

Silence only damages the hearts and minds of the flock. It creates dysfunction of many kinds between the people and the priest. It erodes the trust parishioners once had for the priest. The end result is change in the culture, a lack of interest to participate in church activities, church ministries, or in generosity of monetary contributions. In the hearts of parishioners, it may influence their belief in Christ Himself. Although the priest on the altar may have had no part in the abuse, and may not have known about the credible allegations of diocesan priests, some parishioners will still hold their own pastor accountable because the priest is part of the diocesan organization.

Dysfunction of this nature needs be addressed in church communities just as it is addressed in healthy families. It is hard moments like this that beckon to be shared by priests and parishioners. It is an opportunity to become closer, to forgive, to reenergize, and to move forward, heal, and grow the Church. Addressing the dysfunction is one of the essential ways we will grow the Church by restoring trust.

The priest may think there is not a barrier with the parishioners because he has friends in the parish. Friends or not, this topic needs thorough discussion for trust to be fully restored. This includes with the youth, who analyze the adult world and look for role models, and they know what is going on.

One way to address the issue is with identification repentance followed by a Mass. This method is a new technique and has been done for cities, counties, and government bodies where covenants were broken, resulting in crippling economies and lackluster communities. Dr. John Benefiel writes about this in his book *Binding the Strongman over America* (Benefiel Ministries, Oklahoma City, OK, 2012). This book does not give examples applied to churches, and it is not the same theology as the Catholic Church, but the concept is useful.

This type of church service or meeting would call for all parishioners to attend. All would be prayerful before the event. The purpose is for purification, deliverance, and cleansing/healing of the parish as a whole. It calls all individuals—those who knew about the abuse, those who did not, those who were directly involved with the abuse, those who sat on the sidelines, as well as the abused themselves or a sponsor filling in for the abused. Identification repentance is to name or identify the broken covenant clearly, repent, renounce the power of darkness, **and** reconcile.

At the beginning of every Mass, we repent and ask for forgiveness for sins committed in thought, word, and deed; for the things done, for things failed to do. If we consider for a moment the motto of St. Philomena: **"Everything happens for a reason and everyone is responsible for what happens." It is not participating in the blame game, but we are the family of God, and when one is broken and one is weeping, we all suffer together**. The outcome is to hit at the root system spiritually. For example, when you are weeding, you take the weed out by the roots so it cannot regrow and continue destroying and draining the life of the garden.

Thus far, the Church has practiced reconciling with investigation, individual financial recompense, and prayer. In order for trust to be re-established, we need to form a new spiritual covenant through Christ with the parishioners to assure commitment, love, and unity. Even so the adage "trust is earned" comes to mind. Through identification repentance, trust instead is given freely until proven wrong. This charitable overture binds the parishioners, staff, and priest/deacons. An attitude of forgiven but not forgotten cleans off the slate, and the congregation can move on. The Church, having paid dearly for the sins committed, allows the Holy Spirit to move freely once again. It requires ownership of the trespasses. Only then can the kingdom "be built on earth as it is in heaven." And as Bishop Robert Barron says, "It is not about you." The bigger picture is building the kingdom of God on earth.

In marriages when covenants are broken, the trust is restored by a promise or proclamation that the covenant will not be broken again. It is sealed by gestures of reconciliation of love. It may be an idea for the bishop to make a promise or proclamation to restore the covenant with his people. This may be welcomed by parishioners from their parish priest as well. It may be in the form of:

I, your bishop or priest promise never to be complicit in my duties to protect my parishioners of all ages. I repent of my dereliction (this may be specifically addressed) and ask for your forgiveness. I give you my oath.

There was much accomplished by cleaning house in the Diocese of Buffalo. Key people in the debacle left their positions and were not reassigned. However, not all of them left. There are still several priests immersed in scandal who are practicing in the Church and in addition, bishop, and other hierarchy such as vicar general and the chancellor who assist the bishop and know about the predator priests. In order to restore trust, the investigations need to be done whilst the priests are out of diocesan practice. This includes any priest connected to scandal or where there is a semblance of truth. Such a practice will greatly show the sincerity of the bishops and greatly help to restore trust for parishes directly connected to scandal or not. All parishes in the diocese suffer from distrust of the hierarchy.

As of April 2020, twenty-three priests in the Diocese of Buffalo with substantiated allegations against them have lost their financial and health benefits. Measures such as this will help restore trust in the Catholic system.

Lastly, there is another matter of reconciliation. The Child Victims Act enables a financial reconciliation to be made, which includes counseling services for the victims and their families. There is yet another reconciliation to be made, one of a spiritual nature. Praying for the victims has become commonplace. Perhaps a rite of some kind can be created to restore the heart and soul of the abused. This is said not to undermine in any way the power of the Sacraments. But the offenses committed against the victim were committed by a priest, who stands in the place of Christ Jesus. This means the impact is deep and at the very heart of the soul. The demons linger for years to come, even after reconciliation. The rite may be in the form of purification and purging through the power of the Holy Spirit all of the demons connected with the offense so that the victim is freed and healed. In other words, the result of the abuse may be continued spiritual warfare upon the soul of the victim. The spiritual warfare is through no fault of the victim. Still, the demons linger and hound.

What about the priest offender? A Mass was held by and for them, led by Bishop Edward B. Scharfenberger, the interim bishop administrator at a church in Buffalo, New York. This led to an uproar from the parishioners in the diocese. Why was this? The parishioners were offended that the predator priests were allowed on the altar and to be part of the consecration of the Holy Mass. The bishop explained that it was a private Mass for priests not in good standing with the diocese, and that under Canon Law such priests are allowed to celebrate the Mass. It was a Lenten Mass that was not public but "intended to convey the mercy and grace of God for all who seek forgiveness and the assurance that our brokenness—our grave moral and spiritual failings—do not alone define us as His daughters and sons," spoken by Interim Bishop Edward B. Scharfenberger (Catholic News Service reported in March 2020).

The bishop explained that if a priest is laicized, he may not celebrate the Mass. No excommunication was identified or in place. However, this was an example of the parishioners' hardened hearts, because trust had not been restored.

EXCOMMUNICATION

The practices of the early Church are exemplified in Paul's First letter to the Corinthians. Persons were ex-communicated as a "medicinal penalty." This seems less practiced today. Excommunication, according to John P. Beale in his book *A New Commentary on the Code of Canon Law* (page 63), invites the person who incurred the penalty to change behavior or attitude, to repent, and to return to full Communion with the Church. Excommunication communicates a loss of rights, such as the right to the Sacraments. But the excommunicated are still bound to the obligations of the law; their rights become restored when they are reconciled through the remission of penalty. Meanwhile, the excommunicated Catholic is forbidden from receiving any Sacrament and is refused Catholic burial. The excommunicated is still bound by canonical obligations such as attending Mass or fasting seasonally. An excommunicated Catholic is barred from receiving the Eucharist or from taking an active part in the liturgy like the reading or bringing up the gifts. They are still Catholics, but they are separated from the Church. In Roman Catholic Canon Law, excommunication is the censure intended to invite the person to change.

Scott Hahn talks about excommunication as a gift to priests, bishops, and cardinals, so they may repent and change their ways. It is for the good of the soul.

Those in the public eye, such as politicians who encourage practices against Roman Catholic doctrine, can be excommunicated. The practice helps to prevent corruption of the flock. For example, "Pope Francis ex-communicated the Italian Mafia in 2014. Even Napoleon was not above Canon Law on excommunication. Juan Parone and Fidel Castro are reported to have been excommunicated." (Wikipedia, "Excommunication in the 20th and 21st century.")

As many as two dozen cardinals throughout history have been excommunicated. Bishops and the Pope may excommunicate. There are many reasons for excommunication. Some are for starting up a new church, for accusing the Pope of heresies, for extortion from the Church, and for illicit ordinations. Members from an organization in the Church can be excommunicated. An example of this is the Diocese of Lincoln, Nebraska, where members were excommunicated for promoting positions incompatible with the Catholic Faith such as with Free Choice, Planned Parenthood, the Hemlock Society, and the Freemasons.

Leaders giving speeches against papal policy may be excommunicated, as happened to Father Romolo Murri, leader of the Italian Catholic Democrats. In 2012, in Uruguay, the Bishops' website explained the automatic excommunication would apply under Canon Law 1398 to anyone carrying out an abortion and not to lawmakers of abortion. A priest in Cleveland, Ohio, was excommunicated for violating the terms of his leave of absence by setting up a worshiping community. A priest in Bauru, Brazil, and another in Melbourne, Australia, were excommunicated because of refusing a direct order from the bishop to retract statements on same-sex marriage and ordination of women. All of these examples can be found easily in public documentation such as Wikipedia.

FELONS SERVE TIME

Priests typically are laicized but not excommunicated. This means they have been "de-robed" or "defrocked" lost their privileges to practice as a priest. In the past most priests have managed to avoid a criminal investigation and therefore, have not been required to serve time.

According to a large study done by the Associated Press (October 4, 2019), almost 1,700 priests were investigated that were accused of sexual abuse and were found to be unsupervised. This study by AP News was done in October 2019 and is available online. The priests had been released from clerical duties. Over the nine-month research by the Associated Press, priests were tracked down by scouring public databases, court records, property records, social media, etc. The results were astounding.

Hundreds were found to be working in positions of trust and authority, including jobs that dealt with children in Disney World, community centers, family shelters for domestic abuse, and criminal justice programs. Some of the priests had adopted and fostered children. All of the priests in the study had been found to be guilty of sexual abuse.

However, without a criminal record or fingerprinting, no responsible organization would know their history. Three quarters of the total list still served in some capacity in the Roman Catholic Church. As many as 110 had moved out of the country to practice as Catholic priests in good standing in Peru, Mexico, the Philippines, Ireland, and Colombia. There had been no barrier, no means to alert or stop them from practicing.

Some of the list of 1,700 predator priests acquired state board licensing to work with children as counselors and teachers. A few priests were found to be excommunicated from the Roman Catholic Church when they refused to stop participating in other religious activity. This study uncovered that the dioceses do not track laicized priests, or if the priest chooses to take a leave of absence. It is both time-consuming and expensive to do so, which are the typical reasons not to maintain.

One would conclude that predator priests need to be brought before civil court because without criminal convictions, there is no record to lodge tracking of the predator. This conundrum does not protect parishioners or society at large. We have to do a better job at this in order to restore the trust.

If priests are criminally convicted after a proven credible offense is uncovered by the Church, the laicized priests may be tracked on the National Register of Sex Offenders and by state registers to safeguard the community. Criminal convictions do not happen as a common practice and should to restore trust. "You do the crime, you do the time." Such consequences may discourage these crimes from happening. Furthermore, the government is tracking them. It is one less responsibility for a diocese because it takes up a great deal of time and resources. This glaring oversight or loophole needs to be closed in order to restore the trust of the people.

If priests are excommunicated, they may not receive the Sacraments or participate in the Mass, but they may still participate in some capacity in church ministries and attend church, though they may not hold leadership roles. They cannot practice as a priest in any capacity in the Church elsewhere in the world, because excommunication is documented. This would also restore trust.

There is also the issue of parishioner anger and dismay throughout the world, beyond what we observed in our diocese. The people feel betrayed, deeply grieved, and angry at the extent of the crimes, and that the system is still not fixed. Parishioners are angry that the priests are not paying for the crimes themselves, but the money for the lawsuits is coming out of the pockets of parishioners and insurance companies. Typically, the priest does not go to jail but is only laicized.

Therefore, for all of the aforementioned reasons in this chapter, it is recommended that convicted predator priests should be punished with excommunication and criminal litigation, which would include listing them on the National Register for Sex Offenders, on state registers, and requiring that they serve jail time.

CORRECTING POLICY

As of the time of writing this book, MRT (Movement to Restore Trust) made a very helpful discovery that will also help to restore trust in the diocese of Buffalo. This is from their report on the MRT website:

> As noted in a December 2018 America Magazine article, different dioceses and religious orders use differing language ("substantiated," "credible") and definitions. "And in fact, although the DOB (Diocese of Buffalo) uses both "credible allegation" and "substantiated allegation," neither is well-defined in the Diocese of Buffalo policy. In addition, there should be differing standards for determining what needs to be investigated, what is appropriately shared with the public and what results in canonical delict consequences for an accused priest. After a review of the policies from the dioceses of several other cities (Albany, Boston, Charleston, Cincinnati, etc.) it is apparent that the Buffalo policy is lacking in direction and clarity—it is too ambiguous, therefore leaving too much to interpretation."

b. Clearly define and publicly communicate the standard for Triggering the Preliminary Investigative Process As stated in the America Magazine article: "Canon law (the universal legal code of the Catholic Church) does not use the language of credible or substantiated but instead mandates the investigation of any offense against church law 'which has at least **the semblance of truth**.'" See Canon 1717, sec.1.

Movement to Restore Trust (MRT) recommends that the Diocese of Buffalo Policy clarify the standard of proof for initiation of a preliminary investigation using language recited in the policies of other dioceses which have their basis in Canon 1717, sec 1. For example, the policy of the Diocese of Charleston contains the following definition: "1.22 Semblance of Truth: The criterion that distinguishes an allegation as not manifestly false or frivolous. If an allegation has a semblance of truth, it triggers the preliminary investigation." (p 10) In addition, the Archdiocese of Boston policy states that "The Archbishop will decree the initiation of a preliminary investigation when a complaint of child abuse by a cleric has at least the semblance of truth. (Canon Law 1717)." (p 65)

The Movement to Restore Trust (MRT) organization has a comprehensive grasp of what needs to be done in the diocese to ensure transparency throughout diocesan parishes, require accountability and best practices for managing the diocese organization including for child and adult abuse charges, and financial management.

The framework was developed by the skills of one hundred and fifty talented and highly educated Catholics who also studied best practices of other dioceses. The Independent Diocesan Review Board will include laity. They look forward to working with the new bishop when he is appointed to the Buffalo diocese. The participation and oversight of laity will ensure transparency and accountability. This is expected to inject trust into the diocese in a highly significant way. This will restore trust in the Catholic parish.

Throughout salvation history, man has broken covenants with God. We continue to break covenants with God when we break the ten Commandments. Divorce is at an all- time high as we break covenants with each other. Medical doctors take an oath but sometimes do the patient harm due to carelessness. We are an imperfect creature. Prelates and priests are no exception. If a covenant can be restored, every effort should be taken to mend it. The diocese needs to help priests find ways to mend the broken covenants and assure the parishioners harm will not occur again. Obviously, this cannot occur with predator priests because they are not curable. But those priests affiliated with the problem might consider assuring parishioners in creative and meaningful ways. For this to occur there needs to be meaningful and honest communication from the priests to the parishioners. It means being vulnerable and humble, open and repentant. It will help to restore trust in the Catholic parish.

By our baptism, we are called to restore trust. Help us Lord in our brokenness. We grieve for your Church. Help us to forgive. Through the power of Your Holy Spirit, You will lead us into restoration. We give you praise and thanksgiving for your faithfulness and endless love.

CHAPTER 8

WISDOM TO GROW DISCIPLES AND EVANGELISM

Wisdom is the soundness of an action or decision with regard to the application of experience, knowledge, and good judgment. The Bible takes it a little further by coupling it with knowledge of what is right and wrong and with reverence and respect for God, waiting on His counsel.

"The wisdom of this world is folly to God" (1 Corinthians 3:19).

James 1:5 tells us that if you ask for wisdom, "God will give it generously without finding fault."

James 3:17 "But the wisdom from above is first pure, then peaceable, gentle, open to reason, full of mercy and good fruits, impartial and sincere."

Proverbs 2:6 "For the Lord gives wisdom: out of His mouth come knowledge and understanding."

Proverbs 1:5 "Let the wise hear and increase in learning and the one who understands obtain guidance."

This brings us to three more topics. All of them concern building strong disciples, resulting in greater evangelization.

Wisdom would tell us to begin with prayer and to pray all the way through. Firstly, our study found that the parishes that practiced Adoration of the Blessed Sacrament had the most engaged parishioners. Some began Adoration with only one day or two half days and expanded through the week. The largest parishes had perpetual adoration for most of the week. Imagine the wondrous power and wisdom of His Holy Presence. We observed that these parishes were also the most developed and productive. It is also true that, as parish ministries develop, more people are available to expand adoration hours.

The priest can have a great impact in growing adoration by explaining to parishioners why it is so important, how to use time in adoration, and beckoning them to participate. Sit with the Lord and listen.

A list of prayer requests may be printed out for praying during adoration. It may include projects, meetings, and programs underway at the parish. Prayer is the backbone of the Church and the Christian life. Consider the story of Peter in captivity by Herod, in Acts chapter 12. The people prayed unceasingly to God for Peter, and the results are mind-blowing.

Secondly, when a new ministry, program, or capital expenditure begins, it requires a committee. Members need to be chosen from a body of experts, professionals, and strong believers, those known for their communication skills to add to the committee dialogue. For many reasons, this is the body of wisdom that should commence before any project or program is launched.

Thirdly, each member of a parish committee or at-large should be required to pray the Rosary every day, and each committee meeting should begin with prayer for the intentions of the project or program.

The committee in their wisdom begins with a pilot project to test it out. It is a small version of what it may become. This way it limits capital expense and human effort. It gives the parish time to buy into the concept, to give feedback, and decide whether they want to support it or not, like a partnership would. If there is acceptance and approval by the majority of parishioners, they are asked to contribute time, talent, and treasure. In support of a growing project or program, the pastor can ask parishioners to give money or time. Every member of the parish is enlisted.

Once the program is well established and ready for more volunteers, there will be those parishioners that feel unsure about the task or how to participate. There is a technique that can be used that actually would apply to any ministry. It is the concept of job shadowing or what we may call ministry shadowing, where one is under the mentorship of another minister. This builds confidence and eases any anxiety the parishioner volunteer may have.

Then, when the pastor asks for service from each parishioner to serve for six months to a year, the ministry will meet with higher participation and reduce the risk of attrition. Cards can be left in the pews to be filled out or completed online on the parish website.

The project or program should be described always in terms of the parish vision and mission, and should be often repeated after Mass, in the bulletin, and on the website. This allows the parishioners to develop a connection with the parish and lets them know why they are serving. Once the project or program is described, the how is identified: how it is different from past products and how it will be conducted or offered. The how includes: *how it will make people feel and do better as Christians*. This sells it. The why, the how, and the what are simple rules of marketing but can be applied to growing the parish and ministries.

The parishioners and the "unaffiliated," sometimes called the "unchurched" or the "nones," may learn what they can do to take advantage of the project or program and where to connect by word of mouth, website, or via social media. Why do we need wisdom for this? We need wisdom because too often the best plans are not communicated to parishioners, and they are not sold well. You need to sell it for buy-in.

If parishioners think a new program is the "same old, boring, Catholic stuff," it will be dead in the water before it even begins. All these methods assist in changing the culture of the parish. Additionally, have the committee report back on parishes where the same project or program was done well. Bring in some of the experts, those experienced from successful parishes.

Hire only the best staff and do not "give the job to someone you know who needs a job," as recommended by Father Michael White, well known writer of the *Rebuild* books on growing parishes. Here is more of his advice: Look for individuals outside of the parish or within that have the necessary education and training, knowledge of the parish, a heart for the parish, and experience. A good communicator with a sense of humor is a bonus. Maturity in Christian faith is another essential, as well as a person required to be available on weekends and happy to do so. If a ministry has not been thriving, then replace the leadership; if the grace is gone, it is time to move on.

Team or committee meetings are essential on a weekly basis. It can be done virtually with reports and handouts scanned to the other attendees to read before the meeting time. Even a 45-minute meeting can be productive, but more important these meetings allow fellowship and trust to grow. Using Robert's Rules of Order for the purpose to conduct the business part of meetings in an efficient and predictable manner can be very useful in focusing the group, managing information, and coming to a consensus. Assign the role of time keeper and use itineraries to keep the group on task if it is necessary to get more work done. Keep prayer part of the meeting so as not to get into the busyness and secularizing of meetings. It is hard to progress with meetings just once every month or two.

Many tasks can be done by laity to lessen the administrative burden on the priests. By freeing up the priest for the most important tasks, it gives him more time for the Sacraments, preaching, and showing up for events and meetings. Father Binoy Davis of St. Matthew's in Charlotte, North Carolina, shares a word of advice to other priests: "Release your power, and empower the laity." He attributes this important factor to the success of St. Matthew's growth.

Making lists of things laity and staff can do creates new ministries and involves present ministry members in functions that perhaps will redefine them. Tasks concerning funerals, like an intake meeting with a family on how the funeral will be designed, from readings to music to the eulogy, can be done by trained laity. Tasks concerning new membership like creating a gifts and skills inventory so the parish office knows who to call or invite to serve is another useful function. Another task laity can perform is to pre-visit the sick or homebound ahead of time to update the priest before his next visit.

If you find a naysayer in the group meeting or ministry, try to work with the individual to find out what they are contributing. God is a God of order. There is value in the expression "when the grace is gone, time to move on." Perhaps they are not in a group suitable for their gifts and talents.

St. Matthew's parish had a policy of inviting family, friends, the un-churched, and those who have left the Church. The pews are always full at every Mass (this is not an exaggeration), including three daily Masses and several weekend Masses. Fortunately, they have four priests and six deacons, plus a nun. After Mass, there are always parishioners to answer questions about the parish because the parish makes sure parishioners are well-informed about their parish. This is a nice way to open up conversations about the Catholic faith following the Mass, as questions usually arise from newcomers.

When asked how they would do things differently at St. Matthew's, Father Davis explained they were cranking up spiritual development now in the ministries and in the parish as a whole. It seems there is no stopping this parish. It is **on fire with the Holy Spirit!**

From our research over the past year and a half discovering what works in parishes to grow and heal parishes, here are more recommendations as follows:

Practice Adoration of the Blessed Sacrament as often as possible by inviting weekly from the pulpit and explain why this is important and what to do during Adoration.

Encourage and support networking between ministries to help them grow spiritually and functionally.

Hire only the best, most competent, and spiritually well-rounded individuals.

Bishop Robert Barron imparts this wisdom: "Find the center, know you are a sinner, and realize your life is not about you."

Upon review of this book, I found myself reflecting on the trust I had placed in the Church, and having been raised not to question anything concerning clerical hierarchy, I found myself falling into moments of timidity. I fluctuated for days between temerity and timidity. Then someone brought my attention to the Vatican II call to laity. Prior to 1983, laity had no codified rights as members of the Catholic Church. But in that year, Pope John Paul II formulated the rights of the laity (C 224-231) into Canon Law! Our rights call us to fulfill the mission of the Church, to be a missionary church. The rights are based on the following:

- **Right to Participate Actively in Church Life** (c. 204.1)—The laity can and must take part in Sanctifying, Teaching, Learning and Pastoral roles in the Church.

- **Right of Equality** (c.208)—The laity intrinsically possesses true equality in dignity and action requiring that we all take part in the building of the Body of Christ, qualified by our position as child, lay, or religious ordained, and by function such as teacher, pastor, parent, or missionary in the Church. Up until the change in Canon Law in 1983, the Church operated on a system of social classes that were adopted from the Roman Empire. In doing so, the Church had become self-described as a "society of unequals" (*societas inaequalium*).

- **Right to Express Needs, Desires and Opinions** (c. 212.2 & c.212.3)—The laity are equally endowed with the right to express needs, desires, and opinions on all matters pertaining to the ongoing good of the Church.

- **Right to Initiate, Promote and Sustain Apostolic Activities** (c. 216)—In all actions of building the Church in accordance with Gospel values, the laity has the right and responsibility to undertake, promote, and sustain apostolic activity at all levels.

In addition to the above rights explicitly set forth in Canon Law, the following rights are necessarily implied as corollary rights in order to exercise the rights above:

- **Right to be Informed** (c. 204.1)—Underpinned by the basic right of the laity to participate, the laity, therefore, have the right to be fully informed in all matters of Church operations.

- **Right to be Consulted on the Selection of Pastoral Leaders**—While this right is more implied and encouraged than explicitly acknowledged, the faithful, who are in full communion with the Church, should have an active role in the selection process. This right also has a scriptural foundation in Acts 1:15–26 and Acts 6:1–6. (Provided by MRT)

We are not called to be revolutionaries, particularly in Holy Mother Church. However, it was the influence of the activists in the Buffalo Diocese that shed light on the enormous issues and problems the diocese has. Without them, nothing would have changed.

Lord, we ask You for Wisdom to guide and direct us, to heal and build the kingdom (our parishes) here on earth.

CHAPTER 9

THE MESSAGE

How often have you heard, "I didn't get anything out of the sermon or the homily today"? And another typical comment: "I can't remember what the message was about." One priest commented, "Most people will forget what I said before they leave the church."

Do you think this is a problem? As observers, we thought so. It leads us to believe we have wasted our time, and to think about the lost opportunity to feed those that come to church to be fed by the Word of God. It raises the question: Why can some preachers get the message across, where people are weeping in the pews and some smile praising God in response to the message?

As laity, we do not know much about preaching, though we appreciate that it takes Catholic priests years of studying Homiletics and Scripture. The education of Catholic priests is more than most Protestant preachers obtain in their seminaries. Yet, some Protestant preachers draw larger crowds with successful altar calls that result in changed lives. Why is this and what is missing from Catholic preaching?

There are three types of preaching: expositional, textual, and topical. Most often, Catholic priests use expositional preaching, unpacking the intention of the Scriptural text. The priest helps us to understand the author's intention, when the author wrote the Scripture, and in the context of the society where it was originally preached. Why was the Scripture relevant in that particular time? When priests use expositional preaching, the takeaways should be foremost and clearly understood by the congregation to help them grasp the biblical message. Catholic priests have strong training and education in this type of preaching, which avoids taking Scripture literally when it is not meant to be taken literally.

Textual preaching takes part of the Scripture reading and focuses on one main text. The main idea or verse is expounded on, followed by other minor texts or examples, all relevant to the audience listening. By zeroing in on one thought, it makes it easier for the listener to remember something necessary to take away for living the Good News. This kind of preaching can still have elements of expositional.

The most common and easiest preaching for listeners to follow is topical preaching. It is most common among evangelical preachers. A topic is chosen based on relevance to the audience in the pews. The chosen texts or scriptures are from various parts of the Bible to build and support the message. The preacher relates examples of real life to the

Scripture used in support to change behavior. The objective is to change human behavior, decisions, and choices leading to manifest hope and trust in God. Additionally, topical preaching serves to turn the listener away from sin, encouraging them to live lives of good citizenship as well, based on Christian precepts. The unity of purpose and focus is easier to achieve with topical preaching, according to Denny Prutow, author of *So Pastor, What's Your Point?*

How does Joel Osteen, a nondenominational evangelical preacher of Lakewood Church in Houston, Texas, using topical preaching draw enormous crowds? Most often he focuses on prosperity. It is combined with self-help concepts of right thinking, right living, good choices, tithing, with the promise that "God will prosper you." He is known for weaving Scripture into motivational speaker text that comes with almost a guarantee that God will give anything needed for life or wished for if we but turn to God first. However, God did not promise or assure prosperity for life in this world. Yet Osteen draws enormous crowds who want to hear about the magic bullet for life.

Steven Furtick of Elevation Church in Charlotte, North Carolina, is an evangelical preacher who uses the topical preaching approach. He typically focuses on lack of faith that can cause illness, job loss, and other problems in life. Steve Furtick's sermons are an amalgamation of Christian ideas mixed in with words of faith and prosperity. At the end of the message, there is a sense of hope that things will be all right in life.

As Catholics, we dwell on the gospel of Jesus Christ only. We may be tempted to listen to the many other false gospels because they make us hopeful, feel less worried, and sleep more soundly. However, preaching one truth at the expense of other truths may lead to heresy. In Matthew chapter 7 and chapter 24, Jesus foretold of deceptive gospels distorting His message. In Galatians the apostle Paul warns of false teachers with deceptive words leading believers to destructive ways. The apostle Peter makes the same warning in 2 Peter 2:1–3.

According to Trevin Wax, in his book *Counterfeit Gospels*, there are several counterfeits including the Mystic Gospel, the Churchless Gospel, the Activist Gospel, the Social Club Gospel, and Judgment less Gospel, Moralist Gospel, the Therapeutic Gospel, and the Formalist Gospel.

Father Michael White of Nativity Church, Baltimore, Maryland, has found a solution for sermons or homilies that can become too dry and where the takeaways from the message are unclear. The scriptures are read and reviewed in the Catholic Church on a three-year cycle (A, B, C). The scriptures can seem repetitive, and if the message is not clear, it can be lost on the flock. Father White's solution is to ask two key questions that impact the takeaways. The first is, *What do you want the people to know about the Scripture first?* The second is, *What do you want your audience to do that will impact their life and show the love of God to others?* The result in preaching should look like this:

A.   Here is what I want you (the listener) to know.

B.   Here is what I want you (the listener) to do.

Sometimes the message can be delivered using all three methods of preaching—textual, expository, and topical—but the two takeaways are included and thus clearly understood and wrapped up with a bow to be taken home.

When priests use this method of preaching, Catholic homilies and sermons are relevant and applicable, remembered, and moreover applied to everyday Christian living. It becomes poignant when at the end of the Mass, the priest gives the blessing, he also bids the congregation farewell by saying, "Go in peace and serve the Lord."

Father Larry Richards of St. Joseph Bread of Life in Erie, Pennsylvania, will link God's words of wisdom in the parables to our contemporary family life. People from far and wide listen to his homilies and sermons. For example, Father will say this is what God is telling you in the parable. So now go home and treat your family nice and stop sinning.

Lord God, we lift up to You our good priests who have been demoralized by the scandals and mismanagement by the hierarchy. Please help the diocese with effective reforms and the encouragement of parishioners. Jesus, we trust in You.

CHAPTER 10

THE "NONES"

According to a 2018–2019 Pew study, there is a growing number of the un-affiliated among Christian denominations, comprising all age groups but particularly the Millennials. The "Nones" or unaffiliated has grown to 26 percent of the Christian population (2019) up from 12 percent in 2009.

Millennials who are unaffiliated are now at 40 percent in this age group born between 1981–1996. This will have an enormous impact on church growth as baby-boomers and previous generations pass away.

In 2015, 35 percent of the "Nones" were former Catholics. In order to address a strategy in the parish for drawing the "Nones" back to worship in the Church, one has to understand why "Nones" choose not to come to church. The Pew study lists several reasons in order of their importance.

    a.   Question religious teachings (60%)

b.   Opposition to positions taken on social and political issues (49%)

c.   Dislike religious organizations (41%)

d.   Do not believe in God (37%)

e.   Consider religion irrelevant (36%)

f.   Dislike religious leaders (34%)

The following was contributed by Kathleen McGough Johnson

Philosophically, religion conflicts with the modern ethos of individualism and relativism.

One in four Hispanic Americans claims the dubious distinction of being a former Catholic.

While the reasons for the growing ranks of the "Nones" are many, two stand out:

1)   They do not believe that the precepts of Catholicism apply to their individual lives.

2)   They have not had the benefits of stimulating faith formation, led by clerics and informed lay Catholics.

Although not all of the parishes we visited in our diocese are affected by the wholesale abandonment of the Church by its members, enough are in this trend to raise alarm. What we see happening in our diocese seems representative of what occurs in the Church nationwide.

How did this situation come about? When we compare the Catholic Church of the 1970s and 1980s (our young adult years) to the Church of today, the contrast is stark: the vibrancy and number of ministries, the relevance to contemporary life, monetary contributions to support the work of the Church today are missing. Trust is shattered; faith is weakened. Many Catholics question why they should believe, or why their individual commitment is crucial. There is perceived tension between religion and science, and many believe that Truth is relative. The atmosphere of self-invention is prevalent in every aspect of our lives. How does our Catholic faith fit into that self-centeredness?

In what ways can we convince the "Nones," especially young adults and young families, to return to the Church? In order for the young to appreciate how the Church's teachings have relevance to them, we, the older folks and faithful, must be the teachers who emphasize the Church's historical work to correct injustice. The arc extends from Jesus to the modern advocates of social justice. "Whatever you do to the least of my brethren, you do unto me." When we see something good done in the name of the Church, we are seeing its Truth. We must encourage asking questions and finding answers. We must seek the beauty found in the narratives, the rituals of the Church. Of course, this will require organization and commitment from all of us who are older and can pass on the faith. If we hope to attract and keep the "Nones" and the young, we must be educated ourselves. We are the ones who make disciples. "Each one, teaches one." We should make of our Church a missionary society, according to Bishop Barron. "Love God and love your neighbor." These are the two greatest commandments of them all.

Contributed by Kathleen McGough Johnson

How can we begin to fix the situation that may have been produced by poor catechesis? Is it too late now? We cannot throw in the towel, but must try to restore the trust where we failed our children and our faithful by not offering solutions in a timely fashion. It may be a slow grind, but keep in mind, month after month, we lose the battle and more leave the ranks of the Catholic Faith.

Finding the "Lost Sheep"

Every challenge is an opportunity. Social media should be used extensively to appeal, particularly to the young. The use of social media by reasonable Catholics is absolutely essential to counteract the words of the bigoted, angry, and uninformed on the airwaves.

Give everyone the opportunity to study, reflect, and rejuvenate faith by offering distance learning programs. This may be done by combining families, or couples or all male or all female groups. Small groups make a large parish smaller.

Masses and other services should be broadcast for reception into individual homes where families can worship together but only when Mass in person is not available. Clerics and Eucharistic Ministers must expand programs for visiting the homebound. The focus should be on what brings us together: the spiritual language, the Paschal mystery, the collective experience.

Contributed by Kathleen McGough Johnson

Bishop Robert Barron offers many YouTube video panels of discussion on topics relevant to Millennials about the Faith. This may be reproduced by panels of priests from the diocese on a regular basis answering questions and explaining to the "Nones" about the issues with which they grapple. It may make it easier for "Nones" to approach the individual priests and parishes for information to learn more about the Catholic Faith. Panel discussions may be open to several parishes at a time where a hall is well outfitted with media. Fellowship and refreshments may follow to build connections with other believers.

WE ARE CALLED TO SERVE IN SOME WAY

We can be inspired by the Lord's parable of the talents (Matthew 25:24—30). Three servants were given talents in differing amounts and types. The first two multiplied the resources by using all of their talents. The third one was given only one talent, and he did not use it in any way but instead buried it. The master was very angry and gave the talent of the third to the servant that worked and resulted in multiple productive outcomes. The Lord then cast the slothful and unbelieving servant into the darkness. The Lord's discipline leads one to consider the importance of using what we have been blest with for the building of the Lord's kingdom on earth.

Bishop Robert Barron explains that St. Augustine would say that the meaning of the Holy Trinity, Father, Son, and Holy Spirit, is the essence and being of God. St. Thomas Aquinas: In God, essence and existence coincide. "I am who I am."

> *Help us Lord in our unbelief for we know*
> *You love us. Help us to believe that we*
> *may understand.*

CHAPTER 11

TEACHING THE FAITH

T he word catechesis comes from the Greek meaning "to echo the teaching," meaning the teaching of the faith in an interactive process in which the Word of God resounds between the proclaimer, the one receiving the message, and the Holy Spirit (taken from General Directory of Catechesis). Catechesis takes many forms and includes the initiation of adults, youth, and children, as well as the intentional and systematic effort to enable all to grow in faith and discipleship. Simply said, to put people in communion with Jesus Christ, and learn to proclaim the good news of Jesus to others.

In the listening sessions, we learned that we failed miserably at catechesis when children did not wish to attend Mass, religious education, and later, joining the "Nones when reaching adulthood. This was also at the time after Catholic schools were closed by the diocese.

WHEN WAS CATECHESIS DONE WELL?

When was catechesis done well? It was the fifties, and my entire Dutch Catholic immigrant family from the Netherlands was taught by the nuns of St. Joseph Morrow Park in the Diocese of Toronto, Ontario. I cannot speak for my four brothers, who attended Brebeuf Jesuit High School, but I do recall a deep reverence and awe for the Holy Trinity in the Mass. We were taught to sing with our whole hearts and humbly bring our petitions to God, trusting he would answer.

We were taught to be conscientious about not offending God, because He would not be pleased. We were told the offense to the soul would not bring happiness to self or to anyone else. He was an awesome God with a temper. Moreover, He was a just God that could send us to perdition.

The nuns taught us the positive side, too. God was a loving God, caring and wanting the best for His children. After all, He created the world and everyone in it; surely He had a plan for each one of us. We just needed to offer our lives to Him for the sake of building the kingdom on earth. It could take any form of purpose, from scrubbing floors like Saint Teresa did, or doctoring like Saint Luke did. God can use anyone if we just give Him our heart.

The nuns shed light on all of the Bible stories from creation to the New Testament. They revealed the God of a magnificent creation by drawing our attention to it in geography and the sciences. They showed how He managed the waywardness of His people as they continued to overthrow His salvation plan for them. God was a super-hero implanted in our understanding and imagination.

The nuns spoke frequently about grace. "Grace makes the soul holy," they said, "purity and love... worthy of God's presence." This we strived for daily and became our offering to God with prayers, works of charity, and penance.

One of the most profound miracle was Jesus coming in the Eucharist. He did not leave us as orphans after the cross, but He rose again and is with us through the Eucharist at every Mass ... body and blood, soul and divinity, feeding the mystical body, nourishing the heart and satisfying the soul. Reflected by the Eucharistic Doxology prayer—Through Him, and with Him, and in Him, O God, almighty Father, in the unity of the Holy Spirit, all glory and honor is yours, forever and ever. Perfect love. Perfect unity.

We memorized the catechism, the Ten Commandments, and the Beatitudes. Faith was simple, explainable, and lovely. We knew why we were made, what our purpose in life was, and where we were going after death. We also knew why it was so. The catechism became the vehicle to answer the questions.

Hell was a real place. And we had a choice. We could go with Satan and his demons/fallen angels for eternity, or to heaven, which was more beautiful than what we could see on earth. We were told the beauty of earth pales in comparison to heaven. Colors, sounds, creatures, tastes, smells, nature, knowledge, beyond anything we can attribute to or imagine.

We were sure that Satan was a great deceiver where white was code for black, and evil was fueled by Satan's hatred for mankind. God's love for the human race was real, for a race Satan viewed as sub-quality and inferior to himself.

As children growing up under the tutelage of the nuns, we were grateful to God the Father that He sent His only begotten Son to take human form that we might be saved. By His life, He showed us the Truth, the way and the life through His parables, death on the cross, and His resurrection overcoming death. If we but believe, repent, and call on His name, He will save us.

During the fifties and early sixties, whole families went to Confession before Mass. It was simply a habit. We prayed the Rosary on our knees every evening. Not praying before a meal was considered ill-mannered. Rudeness was punished. God and elders were to be respected. Conflicts were sorted out quickly and peacefully. We had a strong work ethic, and it was required each and every day. Sloth and hedonism did not exist. On television, which was still broadcasted in black and white, the *"Dick van Dyke Show"* best depicted married life, with twin beds in the bedroom because on TV sex was not permitted.

A NEW APPROACH FOR TODAY

"Bring the catechism back" was heard time and again in the listening sessions. Catechesis is done by the faith community and parents now. "Give us tools to do our jobs right," parents begged. Bring in family and small group catechesis. Teach us the faith from the pulpit. Explain how pro-choice and abortion does not fit in with Catholic beliefs. Make us want to go to confession. Inspire love for the Eucharist. Stop intellectualizing the gospel, for you are not speaking to seminarians, and apply the gospel to everyday living. Share real examples where the gospel is shared and lived out with non-believers.

How did the catechism lessons of sixty years ago develop the spirituality of the last generation? From my own experience as a religious education teacher, the Catechism had been abandoned and the booklets for high schoolers were woefully inadequate. The reflections on Scripture simply resulted in Jesus being the answer to every question. The program was so simplistic, it insulted the intelligence of the students, and they responded with apathy and resentment. When the students became seniors, they confessed they had not learned a thing from the entire catechesis program. It had been a lost opportunity to form Catholic adults. Some of these youngsters later moved on to Protestant churches, where they were fed the word of God; some simply became part of the "nones" with no affiliation to religion.

In this new century, the current generation of catechesis has been a wellspring of great developments. We see this in the work of Bishop Robert Barron, Chairman of Evangelization and Catechesis for the USCCB. Additionally, Catechesis of the Good Shepherd (CGS) helps set up contemplative catechesis for children, and is recommended by the Bishop of Memphis, David P. Tally. There are many offerings for family Bible studies today using videos and study books by Ascension Press, Loyola Press, St. Ignatius Press, Our Sunday Visitor, and Ave Maria Press.

A religious education teacher was instructing the children on being quiet in the Mass. She asked, "Now Jacob why do you need to be quiet in church?" Jacob replied matter-of-factly, "Because people are sleeping."

We need Catechesis for all age levels. Even our adults need re-awakening and have forgotten the faith – why we believe what we do. If adults were refreshed we would be able to witness it by the way they pray the Mass, and share their faith. Children would have better role models at Mass. For instance, when many are not responding to the prayers by the priest but seem distracted, and the responses are barely audible in the church.

St. Matthew's Church in Charlotte, NC has developed catechesis on all levels for the family. Here is a list of their development:

- 2020-2021 Program Registration

- Adult Faith Formation

  - Christ Renews His Parish

  - Formed

  - Living Your Strengths

- Rite of Christian Initiation of Adults
- SPRED (Special Religious Development)
- Bridge Religious Education Program
- Children's Faith Formation (Elementary Age)
- Confirmation
- Edge At Home
- Faith and Family Program Volunteer
- Sacramental Preparation
  - First Eucharist Parent Information
  - First Reconciliation Parent Information
- Sunday Preschool and Kindergarten
- Virtual RCIT
- Youth Ministry
  - High School Youth Ministry
  - Middle School Youth Ministry
  - Strengths Quest for Teens
  - Youth Ministry Volunteer

Lord, forgive us for what we failed to do.

CHAPTER 12

THE MASS

RESTORING BELIEF IN THE EUCHARIST

Most people believe God is present through prayer and readings like the Protestants do. How can we restore the basic bulwark doctrine of the Eucharist in the Catholic Church?

In the Mass, eyes are riveted to the cross and Tabernacle and on the sacrifice offered over 2,000 years ago on the cross. This perfect sacrifice of an unblemished lamb, Christ Jesus is remembered during every Mass as we offer the Holy Eucharist to God the Father as Christ offered Himself to God the Father. The perfect sacrifice to God the Father, and we remember His new covenant with us, was made in His blood.

For fifteen hundred years belief in the real presence of Jesus in the bread and wine existed (and for many Catholics continued for another 500 years) which was not challenged until Martin Luther. "Consider how contrary to the mind of God are the heterodox in regard to the grace of God which has come to us . . . They abstain from the Eucharist and from prayer, because they do not admit that the Eucharist is the flesh of our Savior Jesus Christ, the flesh which suffered for our sins and which the Father, in His graciousness, raised from the dead." (St. Ignatius of Antioch, *Letter to the Smyrnaeans,* circa 90 AD).

The real presence of Christ Jesus in the Eucharist was upheld by St. Justin Martyr and documented in the second century:

"This food we call the Eucharist, of which no one is allowed to partake except one who believes that the things we teach are true, and has received the washing for forgiveness of sins and for rebirth, and who lives as Christ handed down to us. For we do not receive these things as common bread or common drink; but as Jesus Christ our Savior being incarnate by God's Word took flesh and blood for our salvation, so also we have been taught that the food consecrated by the Word of prayer which comes from Him, from which our flesh and blood are nourished by transformation, is the flesh and blood of that incarnate Jesus" (St. Justin Martyr, *First Apology,* circa 150 AD).

There are countless documents from the time of the Apostles documenting the real presence of Christ in the Eucharist. We can begin in our own parishes by restoring the faith in the gift of Eucharist our Lord gave to us. We can teach what the nuns taught to the children about reverence, love, and awe for the Eucharist. We can restore some of the prayers in Latin in the Mass. We can teach the catechism to everyone, from the children to the adults. We can place the Tabernacle where it belongs, at the front and center of the church. We can bring back adoration of the body and blood of Christ during the consecration, with the sounding of three bells for each species. This is what is being done in Olean, New York, at the minor Basilica of Mary of the Angels.

The Mass before Vatican II recognized the Truth: God, by His word, creates. He created the earth and the universe by His word, the conception of Jesus in Mary was by His word. He healed the sick by His word. It became easy to believe that Jesus could transform (or transubstantiate) bread and wine into His essence—body, blood, soul, and divinity—all by His word. Like the apostles did in the early Church, this is continued via priests through a documented history of ordination over 2,000 years. Each priest can historically determine the lineage of his priesthood going back to the beginning of the Church.

Latin was the sacred language of worship of the Mass, which was also used since the Early Church. Latin became the sacred language worthy of communicating with the Holy of Holies (*Christus Vincit*, 255). Latin was never banned from the Mass, but became optional, according to Vatican II. Fortunately, we have Latin in a few places in the Mass such as the Agnes Dei, the Sanctus, and sometimes the Gloria.

Intrinsic to the Extraordinary Form of the Mass was adoration of the Eucharist in the monstrance or in the tabernacle, or when the Eucharist was held up reverently for several moments by the priest as the three bells sounded following the words of the Consecration. Every Mass had some Eucharistic adoration experientially pre-Vatican II. There is some semblance of this today in the Ordinary Form of the Mass (or Novus Ordo), but perhaps if more pronounced as was done pre-Vatican II, more attention would be drawn to the Eucharistic presence on the altar and in the tabernacle. It likely would help to restore the Eucharistic faith and devotion.

The story of the last supper or the foreshadowing of the cross and resurrection begins with recalling Palm Sunday when the people greet Jesus entering Jerusalem with palms and chanting, [this is in the Mass only "Holy, Holy, Holy, Lord, God of hosts. Heaven and earth are filled with your glory.] Hosanna in the highest. Blessed is He who comes in the name of the Lord, Hosanna in the highest" (Matthew 21:9), and Psalm 118:25. The Mass acknowledges Christ's presence with the biblical words from Palm Sunday, when Jesus was welcomed into Jerusalem only five days before His crucifixion.

The Eucharist was instituted at the Passover supper, an annual event to commemorate the Israelites' release from bondage in Egypt by God through Moses. It is much like our release from bondage of sin to live eternal life in heaven. But the Mass is not like the Passover meal or the Shabbat. The greatest difference is when Jesus did the most irregular and highly unexpected act when He gave thanks for the bread, blessed it or consecrated it, and said, "This is my body, which will be given up for you." As often as we do this, remember … what Jesus (I) did for the salvation of souls. The same words are said in the Mass over the wine, which becomes His blood by His word. "This is the new covenant in My blood which is shed for many." Jesus pledges a spiritual oath to us with His blood (Mark 14:23–25).

Previous to the Lord's sacrifice on the cross to the Almighty God, we were doomed to death. Jesus made the ultimate sacrifice, giving His life to be nailed to a cross which was His triumph over death and propitiation for all our wrongdoings against God. We remember this in every Mass and give thanksgiving. And in so doing, He comes to us. "My body is real food, and my blood is real drink" (John 6:55). He loves us so much that He wants to be in us and with us. And through us, we are sent out into the world to make disciples of all nations.

The ultimate sacrifice ever made to God was the unblemished lamb called Jesus (Hebrews 9:13–14). Why should we continue the sacrifice of the Mass? God does not need sacrifices, for the ultimate one was made for all ages. "A sacrifice acceptable to God is a broken spirit" (Psalm 51:17). We lift up our hearts as a sacrifice to God in the Mass. Because none of us is perfect, we do this in conjunction with Christ Jesus. "Through signs of adoration and gratitude, supplication and communion so as to cling to God in communion of holiness, and thus achieve blessedness, is a true sacrifice," said St. Augustine. Today, we do not think of life in terms of sacrifices made for God or for others. Today, sacrificing for others is not in our mental framework. But God asks us to do so for the love of others, and to love God with our whole heart, mind, and soul. There is exceeding grace and peace through this means of worship. We profess that Christ did die, rose from the dead, and that He will come again. We expect this to happen and look forward to it. All this we do and remember at each Mass.

Father Dennis Mende, pastor at Holy Apostles parish in Jamestown, New York, attributes the loss of belief in the real presence of Christ in the Eucharist today to our dropping the ball on catechesis or education of the faithful. Better explanations and focus on the real presence of Christ in the Eucharist needs to be taught and reinforced by the priest and religious education staff to all parishioners on a regular basis.

SCRIPTURAL SUPPORT

We can prayerfully consider Saint Paul's words:

1 Corinthians 11:24 "And when He had given thanks, He broke it and said, take, eat. This is my body, which is broken for you. This do in remembrance of me."

1 Corinthians 11:25 "In the same manner, He took the cup when He had supped saying, 'This cup is the new Covenant in my blood. This you do, as often as you drink it in remembrance of me.'"

1 Corinthians 11:26 "For as often as you eat this bread and drink this cup, you show the Lord's death and that He will come again."

1 Corinthians 11:27 "Whosoever shall eat this bread and drink this cup unworthily shall be guilty of the body and blood of the Lord."

1 Corinthians 11:29–34 "He that eat and drink unworthily shall eat and drink condemnation to himself, not discerning the Lord's body. For this cause many are weak and sickly among you and many sleep."

If it is just crackers and grape juice and a memorial, condemnation would not apply. Condemnation can only apply if it truly is the body and blood of Christ. That is why partaking of the Body and Blood of Christ in an unholy manner would bring condemnation upon the individual.

St. John Chrysostom also upheld the doctrine in the fourth century in his statement as follows: (Early Church Fathers upholding Transubstantiation in Their Own Words, Sonja Corbitt, 2018)

"I wish to add something that is plainly awe-inspiring, but do not be astonished or upset. This Sacrifice, no matter who offers it, be it Peter or Paul, is always the same as that which Christ gave His disciples and which priests now offer: The offering of today is in no way inferior to that which Christ offered, because it is not men who sanctify the offering of today; it is the same Christ who sanctified His own. For just as the words which God spoke are the very same as those which the priest now speaks, so too the oblation is the very same" (St. John Chrysostom, *Homilies on the Second Epistle to Timothy,* circa 397 AD).

This further illuminates the concept of transubstantiation through the priest. In the hypothesis of the protestant notion of consubstantiation that is Christ becomes present by the prayers of the parishioners. They do not claim it is the Body and Blood of Christ but that He is present among them through prayer and scripture reading. Their communion is in memory of Christ's last supper. In our communion we offer ourselves with Christ who is the unblemished Lamb to God the Father. It is a form of consecrating ourselves to God on a weekly basis or whenever present at Mass.

This has again profound relevance not only for Catholics, but for other denominations. For if we truly believe in the Eucharist as the body and blood, soul and divinity of Christ to nourish our souls, why would we not run to it every day?

WHAT HAVE YOU GIVEN IN THE MASS?

In the Mass pre-Vatican II, there was a strong sense of gratitude for His presence with prayers of Thanksgiving and petitions. This is still done today but a longer pause to gather one's thoughts may be helpful.

The Mass culminated with receiving the spiritual food and sitting or kneeling in contemplative prayer for several moments. This is afforded when there is a large number of parishioners processing up for communion.

Perhaps there are a few things for consideration to deepen the spiritual experience of the Eucharist. For instance, turning the priest back around to the Tabernacle in front and center for some of the Mass, for example, the Offertory and Canon of the Mass. Bishop Schneider offers many reflections.

Perhaps place the cathedra or priest's chair to the side of the altar and not in the center so that the priest's face is not watched all the time. Jeremiah 32:33, "and they have turned to me the back and not the face."

Sometimes older children complain they get nothing out of the Mass. I always ask, *What have you given in the Mass that you are not getting anything out of it? Did you do any of the following?*

Repent for your sins at the beginning of the Mass?

Hear the meaning of the word of God when the scriptures were read?

Lift up your heart to God at the offeratory?

Did you put yourself on the altar with Christ Jesus when He is being offered to God as a memorial sacrifice?*

Did you affirm that He is the son of God in the Body and Blood raised up to God?

How often did you praise Him throughout the Mass?

Who did you pray for during the Mass? For yourself or for others?

How often did you thank Him?

Did you tell the Lord you love Him?

*The celebration of the Eucharist which takes place at Mass is the action not only of Christ, but also of the Church. For in it, Christ perpetuates in an un-bloody manner the sacrifice offered on the cross, offering himself to the Father for the world's salvation through the ministry of priests. The Church, the spouse (the lay faithful) and minister (priest) of Christ, performs together with Him the role of priest and victim, offers him to the Father and at the same time makes a total offering of herself together with him. (Taken from *Eucharisticum Mysterium Vatican II* documents, 25 May 1967, introduction paragraph 3).

Thus, the Mass is very interactive and active with God and with fellow parishioners. There is no time for boredom, distraction or side tracking. The Mass can be viewed as one continuous prayer, homage and veneration to God Almighty, to Jesus and to the Holy Spirit. Prayed from the heart it is total immersion in the act of worship. It is the second commandment prayed out "Love the Lord your God with your whole mind, heart, soul and strength.

Bring the sanctuary lamp back to the Tabernacle that signifies God is present. This is not visible at the tabernacle in some parishes. This concept originated in the days of Moses when God asked that a lamp be lit at the Ark of the Covenant at all times, and so olive oil burned there at all times as a reminder that God was present. In this age, the lit eternal lamp is meant to be before the tabernacle of the new covenant with God Almighty, which is Jesus Christ, denoting that He is present in the tabernacle.

The Catholic Church in Charlotte, North Carolina, St. Matthew's Church, has a recording of Gregorian Chants played softly before the Mass. It may be offered following the Mass, which presents the atmosphere of holy adoration. This may be a very nice addition for our parishes.

Perhaps we could consider bringing back the altar railings for those who wish to receive on the tongue, post-Covid era. This makes Communion less of a cafeteria style as recommended by Bishop Schneider. If not, the faithful should be encouraged at least to genuflect or bow deeply before receiving the Eucharist. This gesture recognizes the holiness of the Eucharist and of the act of receiving the Eucharist. It is not crackers or bread and grape juice.

Perhaps not have a display of the sign of peace with fingers in the shape of a V or waving broad communal greetings just before receiving Christ, which breaks the reverie for some parishioners, and the reverence of the prayers preceding Communion. Perhaps this can be done at the opening of the Mass when the priest greets the people.

MUSIC AND DRESS CODE

Music draws people into worship. In the protestant churches music may be the major part of the service followed by a message and prayer. Sometimes the music is transformative when it is praise music from the heart to God. Here are some very good ones which may be incorporated into the Mass and may especially appeal to the youth for the youth Mass.

1. Bless the Lord Oh My Soul

2. What a Beautiful Name It Is

3. How Great is Our God (in different languages of the congregation)

4. Holy

5. Blessed Be Your Name

6. Never Once

7. I worship you my God

8. We Praise You

9. Abide With Me

10. Ten Thousand Reasons for My Heart To Sing

11. Greatest Hallelujah

The Protestants have made music one of the pillars of their faith, a cornerstone of the worship service. They have clearly evidenced the importance of this as a form of prayer and worship. We need to consider some of their music because many of our Catholic hymns are tired, hard to sing and difficult to relate to the lyrics. This industry certainly has room to explore creative ways and means to develop Catholic worship music.

On our visits to parishes in the Diocese of Buffalo, we found marked differences in the vestments of the altar servers. Some had messy street shoes or dirty running shoes that peeped out from unpressed vestments. In most churches, some altar servers said none of the prayers, while others attempted to pray but perhaps did not know the prayers completely.

The vestments at St. Mary's in Swormville, New York, were white with green surplice (upper and outer vestment). Pleasing to the eye, it gave the appearance the children were well cared for and trained. It was a similar effect as the black cassock with white surplice worn in the fifties and sixties. At Sacred Heart Church in Lakewood, New York, the altar servers wore short red capes which gave a Vatican appearance and was also impressive. The altar servers at Our Lady of Loretto wore a green surplice with an old style cross hung over the front, in keeping with the Tuscan style, stone structure of this exceptionally beautiful church in Falconer, New York.

We thought that the garb worn on the altar was important because of the attention given to the assistants on the altar, as well as the importance of prayerfulness of the assistant. This included cantors, lectors, and Eucharistic ministers. Too much attention is drawn to women's fashion and shapes on the altar. It is a distraction from the holiness of the Mass. All ministers need to wear liturgical garb. We saw this in Charlotte, North Carolina. They also had name tags for ministers so they were greeted by name.

John 4:24. God is a Spirit. And they that worship Him must worship him in Spirit and in Truth.

The culture of this century is ultra-casual even in the Mass with teenagers coming in short shorts and back-less tops. The purpose of the Mass is to give praise and thanksgiving to God and to become more holy ourselves if we take heed of scriptural messages. Without Catholic schools and nuns correcting children, they seemed to have lost the course on this note. The nuns would tell us not to *distract the boys from their time with God.*

In the name of the Father, and of the Son, and of the Holy Spirit, Amen. How did we as Christians stop making the sign of the cross? It is a salutation and a closing of communication with God. It is by the cross we are saved. How is it we are embarrassed about it? God does not change, we do. There was once gratitude, pride, love, joy, and honor in making the sign of the cross.

> *By your cross and resurrection, You have set us free. Help us now to grow in Christ Jesus through the fellowship of the Holy Spirit, Amen.*

CHAPTER 13

POST-COVID 19 CHURCH

This chapter closes with future scenarios following the scandals in the Diocese of Buffalo, and the next shoe that fell when the Covid 19 pandemic hit the world. It is important to envision the impact of the pandemic on future church attendance. The suggestions throughout this book will help to circumvent the attrition that is bound to occur.

In March 2020 the entire Diocese of Buffalo became sequestered. People were prevented from attending Mass and ministries because of a mandatory shutdown by governors throughout the nation to prevent the spread of a highly contagious virus Covid 19. With the exception of essential services such as grocery stores, hardware stores, drug stores, beer and alcohol stores, and gas stations, society shut down, and so too did the churches. Not even the last rites were administered in hospitals for Catholic parishioners. (There did not seem to be a fight for establishing church as an essential service, either.)

Some Catholic parishes began video-taping the Mass via Zoom or Go To Meeting. Many people watched the Mass on TV via EWTN, or Bishop Robert Barron, and many other Masses on YouTube which consisted of a priest and lector, and a better than average message or homily. A prayer at the end of the Mass for Spiritual Communion was provided on the screen. The church lockdown continued for more than four months in the Diocese of Buffalo. This was followed by a partial opening for about 30 percent capacity lasting months to the date of this publication.

Although, Mass may be attended in person wearing a mask, many parishioners choose to continue the convenience of watching Mass from their living room. Combined with the high percentage (70 percent) Catholics who do not believe in the real presence of Christ in the Eucharist, this may be a bad combination of practices that may affect Mass attendance in the near future. The shepherd will need to guide the flock away from this cliff.

Add to the above scenario the new culture in our Church following the sex scandals and lack of trust in the hierarchy of the Church. It would seem that attendance will continue to free fall as it has done for the last few years unless real change happens.

Moreover, the history of poor catechesis and lack of family support for spiritual growth in our parishes means there are more reasons for parishioners not to return.

For some parishes, weekly contributions from parishioners dropped by 30 to 50 percent after the sex scandals reached the media. Giving further declined for some parishes when Covid 19 closed their doors. It could still decline further if people switch to other denominations.

Add more stress to the situation with the growing shortage of priests due to many factors, including retirements and priests taking leave of absence or sabbatical. This leads one to recognize the crisis must be dealt with immediately.

THE PATH FORWARD AND PITFALLS TO AVOID

The following is contributed by Kathleen McGough Johnson

In the future, when we are able to resume some semblance of normalcy in our worship, these are a few recommendations for the post-Covid 19 Catholic Church.

To all healthy adult parishioners: volunteer to aid the ill and elderly through mercy ministries such as distributing food, clothing, medicines, even bringing the Holy Eucharist. Christian charity heals wounds while bringing others into the fold. Father Mark Noonan, St. John Vianney, Orchard Park, New York, encourages through his bulletin, "St. John Vianney provides the ultimate example of what our Church and world need right now. It needs renewal, conversion, mercy, charity, holiness and faith. It needs those things from each and every one of us."

To devout lay people educated in how to be successful at teaching faith formation: volunteer to be a mentor to a

RESTORING TRUST IN THE CATHOLIC PARISH

young person or a young family. Establish a catechesis program that teaches discipleship so everyone mentors someone. As disciples are made, the Church strengthens and grows and so does evangelism.

To lay women: encourage, give opportunity, expect that lay women will assume responsibility for faith formation classes, for work in other ministries, for management—outside the clerical sphere—of their parishes. The same can be said to men because the Church is in need of upright male role models, especially to the youth.

To young adults and young families: seek willing lay-people to mentor you.

To the prelates: make the Church visible as it ministers to those who cannot care for themselves. Draw strength from the Holy Spirit in these difficult times. Be a strong parent to your priests, for they hold the souls for Christ in their care.

Stage open-air Masses in football/soccer fields, weather permitting. It breaks the pattern of worshiping in the same place. Bring in celebrity priests to preach the gospel and use large screens. This can kick off a one day retreat. Or instead of an outdoor Mass, have the speakers join with a Christian rock band to kick off a retreat.

Use social media to teach and evangelize, making it relevant for people to want to log on to the parish website at least once per week or more for the whole family.

Understand that out of traumatic experience, we often emerge stronger, more resilient. This is your opportunity to restore hope and make an impact.

Encourage confession made to God in prayer, when a face-to-face meeting with the confessor is not possible. Repentance and reparation is good daily practice, and good for the soul.

For all of us Catholics: look to history to learn how in time of plague, when governmental infrastructure failed, it was the Christians who tended to all the poor and the ill, with grace and dignity. In his book Catholicism in the Time of Coronavirus, Dr. Stephen Bullivant explains that humanitarian values and "do unto others as you would have them do unto you" were born in Christianity. Look at the lives of the saints to find role models of perseverance, kindness, selflessness; copy their behavior in the face of hurt and disillusionment. "I can do all things through Christ who strengthens me" (Philippians 4:13).

Focus on the belief that this pandemic provides the opportunity for a greater good to occur. If we trust in the Lord, He will show us the way. The Venerable Fulton Sheen gave us just two words to remind us of our duties as Catholics: "Come," as in "Come unto me" for grace, spirit, peace; and "Go," as in "Go into the world to proselytize, baptize, bring together."

Be grateful for others, the ordinary, quiet heroes who serve our communities without asking for reward. Be kind to all.

Contribute—as much as is possible—to the many ministries struggling to accomplish their work during the pandemic. We may consider expanding to include a wider range of musical styles, such as classical, jazz, reggae, in addition to the traditional liturgical music. Use praise music that appeals to one's spirit, singing from the soul. In proclaiming the glory of the Lord, instruments like drums, horns, and strings add immeasurably to piano and organ. Choirs, too, can adapt to a change of rhythm.

The whole congregation should be encouraged to sing loudly. The priest has the most impact on this request. Facilitate by using large screens with large print.

For those who are skeptical of priests who have committed unseemly acts but still remain in the Church, bear in mind that the goodness of the Sacraments stands on its own, regardless of the goodness, or evil, of the Sacramental minister.

To prelates: Most essential, offer a strong spiritual guidance program to priests, where every priest has a spiritual advisor and guide that is outstanding at meeting the needs of the priest.

Contributed by Kathleen McGough Johnson

To priests: lead from the back and let others believe they are in front. A good leader demonstrates humility. A priest is like a shepherd. He stays behind the flock, letting the most nimble go out ahead, thereupon the others follow, not realizing that all along they have been directed from behind, letting others shine and feel their value. Watch sheepherding sometime. A shepherd has assistance on the sides with the help of well-trained dogs, but he calls the shots from a distance, including organizing the herd.

Keep the vision in front of everyone, and follow the steps of the mission as you recognize that your goals come to fruition. Do this for your Church as a whole and for each ministry.

Introduce and use the "Living Your Strengths" program on your website so that everyone may join a small group to discern gifts, talents, in the Church, (if called to ministries), and skills to use in everyday life.

Find ways to work with people where they are at in their faith journey. Fr. Darrell Duffy of Jamestown, New York, gives Communion to the parishioners in the parking lot after they have prayed his Mass on Zoom. Once Covid 19 is cleared from the population, this offering likely will become unavailable.

Others in the nation have drive-up confession. This service was established in other parishes specifically in Wisconsin prior to Covid. If electronic means is not used, it does not break the seal of confession.

There is a wide variety of offerings and strengths in Catholic parishes in a diocese. If you are seeking faith formation and edification for your children, find a parish that meets your family needs, even if it means you have to travel a far distance or even move to another city. Or get a group together and make it happen in your own parish.

If your priest is willing to enlist the laity to help develop the parish to meet the growing needs of parishioners, offer your time, talent, and treasure to build the kingdom for Christ Jesus, and free up the priest to administer the Sacraments which the laity cannot do. Recognize the priest runs the church, but you can have great influence for good, and moreover, by Canon Law instituted by Pope John Paul II in 1983, it is your right to do so.

Your church needs prayer. Pray the Rosary often. It takes only fifteen minutes. If driving to the grocery store is ten minutes, pray half of the Rosary there and the other half coming back. It may seem repetitive at first, but given enough times, you may discover the truth of the Rosary in that it holds joy and peace. It is somehow another one of God's mysteries. *The Rosary: Spiritual Sword of Our Lady* by Fr. Donald Calloway explains the power of the Rosary over the trials of darkness.

To the Homebound: We look to you to be our prayer warriors. Consider Saint Padre Pio who prayed up to thirty-five rosaries per day!

Following Vatican II, there has developed over time less consideration for the forgotten souls in purgatory, and many Catholics ceased to pray for them personally. This practice and belief had always existed in the Church, but Christianity was impacted by the new views of the Reformation five hundred years ago. In fact, praying for the souls that passed on was a practice and belief in Jesus' time, where the Jews had always prayed for their dead and still do today. The prayer is called the "Kaddish" and "El Malei Rachamim." Catholics pray for the dead because death is considered to be only a change, not an ending of the soul. Catholics pray for the dead at every Mass, On Sunday of Divine Mercy, and on All Souls' Day, because the Body of Christ on earth continues into the afterlife. Muslims pray for their dead to seek pardon for them. Consider how many souls have not been prayed for since the Reformation ... probably billions who could use prayers.

Attend daily Mass. I call it a mini-Mass. It takes less than twenty-five minutes and it is a perfect prayer from beginning to end. It is "give us our daily bread" and centers the day on Christ Jesus and blesses life. Cities offer daily Mass several times a day.

Sit in Adoration of the Blessed Sacrament enough times, and God will answer. Many parishes offer Adoration of the Blessed Sacrament. The strongest parishes are those with perpetual adoration.

Pray for the pope, cardinals, bishops and priests. The powers of darkness are upon mankind, but even greater upon those who are working for the kingdom of Christ Jesus. Since 1950 in the Diocese of Buffalo, 7.5 percent of all priests in the last 70 years in the diocese have denigrated the reputation of the other 92.5 percent of priests. Most priests are good and serve God and his people with their whole hearts. Send a card of encouragement and appreciation to them. These men have been set apart for God and belong to Mary. They have had to struggle within seminaries, dioceses, and community to keep on serving and be faithful to their vows. Please consider lifting them up.

To the dioceses and parishes, stop asking for money, and ask for time and talent instead. The treasure will follow when the parishioners see results.

The pastor said to his congregation, "I have good news and bad news. The good news is that we have the money for developing ministries. The bad news is that it is sitting in your pockets."

The money will continue to sit in the parishioners' pockets until they see results. We need to have answers to the despair, dissatisfaction, and anger in the current Catholic culture.

Reduce fundraising to one major activity and focus on spiritual development of parishioners of all ages.

Return to the knowledge in the Catechism, teaching all ages including the adults.

Hire a male and a female youth leader that can reach out to a number of Catholic parishes in a region. Create youth groups appropriate to age before Confirmation and after Confirmation.

Network with the weaker Catholic parishes that struggle to the point of closing.

Network with your own ministries to help them become effective and joyful. People looking for a parish want to see the joy of the Lord, for it is the life of the parish.

To the Chancery of the Diocese: When parishes ask for financial support and help to turn their parish around in areas of catechesis, youth spiritual development, new ministry, technology, training, planning, please consider a gift of reconciliation by way of financial support. It is a wonderful opportunity to make amends for the wrongs committed by the diocese and a loving gesture to help restore trust!

Invest in the family first and foremost. It is the backbone of the Church. This means child care with catechesis in the nursery. Create a plan to step it up as the parish grows.

Incorporate the youth in parish council, ministries, faith formation, and the Mass. Begin a youth Mass with their involvement and then step it up to weekly youth Masses open to the parish at large.

Tap into the wisdom of the older generation in the parish, and enlist them into meaningful ministries.

Hire competent staff and pay them well and do not take advantage of their good will.

Increase communication with the parishioners by ramping up the website, technology, and various means of disseminating church information, and faith development. This includes an organization chart of all the ministries, including contact persons, scheduled meetings, location of meetings, leadership contact info, projects being worked on, and events so that parishioners can easily see where their schedules can plug in for ministry volunteering.

Require (meaning with much encouragement) everyone to join one small group for three months to learn discipleship and evangelism in meeting rooms on the church campus or in individual homes, with the first one held in the church on a Sunday afternoon.

Take advantage of family Bible studies at home or at the church. Combine families but try to keep it to less than twelve people per group. It is an opportunity for parents to share faith and testimonies with their children.

Darkness has lingered around Mother Church since the beginning of Church history, and it rears its ugly head about every hundred years. The trial today oppressing her is one of the worst, but like the other trials, we will overcome. We will beat this one too because Jesus claimed in Matthew 16:18, "And I tell you, you are Peter, and on this rock I will build my church, and the gates of hell shall not prevail against it."

It is a recommendation that pastors discuss the Church crisis with the parishioners. In addition to adhering to Virtus, the national program for the protection of children, ask that more programs be developed for understanding human sexuality, the practice of chastity, and the meaning of true love.

Throughout the history of sexual scandals in the Church, the punishment has been minimal for convicted predator priests. It has been the parishioners and insurance companies that have had to pay out of pocket for the abuse. It is our recommendation standing with other brothers and sisters in Christ of the same mind that convicted predator priests be punished with excommunication and criminal prosecution. Excommunication and criminal prosecution are preventative and corrective measures which should be used only when the proof of abuse is undeniable. This would help to restore trust again in the Catholic system. It reflects that the Church has changed effectively.

Belief in the Holy Eucharist can be restored again. The Pell study percentage is alarming. And 70% lacking belief is daunting. However, let us keep in mind and be inspired that through a strong catechesis program at St. Matthew's Church in Charlotte, North Carolina, as many as 500 children make first Communion every year! And as many make Confirmation! We should not lose heart but make every effort to correct our ways and means!

During Covid 19 we learned to enjoy home, be a family, do with less shopping and entertainment, and work from home whilst life swarmed around the house. We learned to make sacrifices for the family and for outsiders for their safety, health, and wellbeing. We also became aware, some of us painfully aware, that we need to prepare for disasters better, focus on what is relevant, and meet our challenges in prayerful ways. We also realized that this is not the end of pandemics or national and global disasters. There will be others in our lifetimes, some perhaps even more devastating and with longevity. It behooves us to ask the question: What do we need to do to prepare as a Church so worship, ministries, discipleship and evangelization may continue? It is in crisis that we need the Church the most.

Remember 9/11 when the attack upon our nation brought everyone together and filled our churches? We need to draw together again as Catholics during this crisis in the Church. Our only hope is prayer and the love and mercy of God. Through Christ Jesus and the love of the Father, we will rebuild the Roman Catholic Church to be better than ever. To do nothing is a pitfall in and of itself.

THE WAY OF EUROPE

One of the concerns of Catholics is that our American Church will go the way of Europe, which is to say a rapid decline. If we look at the Catholic Church in the Netherlands, we can glean many helpful hints.

The sex scandals came to a peak in 2010 in the Netherlands only several years ahead of ours. By 2018, half of the cardinals and bishops 20/39 were implicated in the sex scandal cover-up and acted on by Pope Francis, who said he "will take action to end the culture of cover-up" of the sex scandals. Additionally, impunity is not practiced in Europe where Church sex scandals are concerned. Throughout Europe, the British Isles, and Ireland, priests, monks, and bishops are being sentenced to time in jail.

In the Netherlands, since 2010, **25 percent of priests have left** since the massive decline of the Catholic population and church closings. The Dutch cardinal Wim Eijk has predicted that by 2025, **two-thirds of the Catholic churches**

will be closed in the Netherlands. This is both shocking and foreboding for our church in America. As Catholics we should take this omen very seriously and act quickly to repair the trust and the functionality of our parishes.

In the 1960s, **55 percent** of the 2.7 million Dutch Catholics went to Mass regularly. Today, it is **5.6 percent**. In the 1960s, the Catholic Church was culturally important to the community. The parish baptized everyone. Today, one in 11 are baptized, and one in 10 marry. In the Netherlands alone, the fact that 20,000 children since 1950 suffered abuse at the hands of 800 priests, brothers, pastors, lay people, and other clerics reported had an impact on the change in Catholicism (Mike Corder, Associated Press, September 2018).

Life is a faith journey all the way. Consecrate your life to the Holy Trinity and allow yourself to be guided by the Holy Spirit. It is a great beginning to turning the chaos, despair, and disunity around.

There is work to be done in the Church for each and every one at the parish level. Get organized and trained, and call out for everyone in the parish to become involved even for just one year of commitment. Consider the prophetic words of Father Jan Trella of Blessed Mary Angela Parish in Dunkirk, New York, when he said, "Take care of Mother Church. She is sick right now and don't turn away from her. You would not turn away from your own mother if she were ill. Mother Church needs you."

Consider St. Philomena Parish's motto: "Everything happens for a reason and everyone is responsible for what happens." Come together as a church to repent and reconcile. Make a fresh start all the while demanding transparency and accountability. The church belongs to all Catholic parishioners. By canon law it is our right to be involved and be informed. For instance, when emails and letters from the laity and priests are not responded to what does this say? It says the chancery does not care either about the good will or the opinions. Communicate! Tell us what we need to hear not what you need us to hear. This is required in every company, family, and institution. Only then, will the trust be restored! Only together will the trust be restored.

In the region of Limburg, the Netherlands offers us a glimpse of hope for the Church in this crisis. In this southern part of the Netherlands bordering Germany and Belgium, a parish continued to hold on to their devout Catholic culture. The parish had processions through the village to pray and honor saints, Mary, and the sacred heart of Jesus. The parish had wedding celebrations in the church and for feast days, and everyone came. The youth played sports on the parish grounds. Outdoor picnics on parish grounds were frequent on Sundays in the summer. Group retreats, novenas at the parish shrine to Our Lady of Lourdes resulted in healings. Typically, lunch with parishioners would follow Mass at the pub or restaurant nearby. Parishes of other villages would have competitions like who could bring in the longest tree trunk with horse and wagon. Only unmarried men (parishioners) could volunteer. The youth incorporated the traditions of Catholicism into their faith journey and added fun to it. The tree trunk was then planted in a well next to the church. The branch-less trunk with the exception of the pinnacle, towered next to the stone church signifying prayers ascending with the goal all should aspire to heaven's domain.

The Catholic culture is still intact in Limburg because Archbishop Wim Eijk, now cardinal, asked that devout older Catholics take small groups of families and youth, and teach them the Faith.

The Catholic culture has an understanding there that Catholics can laugh about the Church, realize there are good Catholics and bad ones, good priests and bad ones. Moreover, there are many traditions, richness in the Faith that take a lifetime to experience and understand. (From the documentary *Anthropology of the Dutch Catholic in the Netherlands* by Michael Schaap als De Hokjesman, 2017.)

When it comes to the spiritual, 1 Corinthians 13:13 advises, "These three remain: Faith, hope and love, abide these three; but the greatest of these is love." Help to create the Church so that you and your family may abide in faith, hope, and love. Make it better than imaginable. Help save the Church because Jesus saved you first.

> "*Who is going to save our Church? Not our bishops, not our priests and religious. It is up to you, the people. You have the minds, the eyes, and the ears to save the Church. Your mission is to see that your priests act like priests, your bishops act like bishops, and your religious act like religious.*"

Archbishop Fulton J. Sheen (Speech to the Knights of Columbus, June 1972)

We have only a few years left if Europe is any indication of what is in store for us in our Catholic dioceses.

✝

At the end of our research journey and only after our book *Restoring Trust in the Catholic Parish* was finished, I realized it had called for a paradigm shift in the diocese, in order for the Church to restore and rebuild trust and allow parishes to grow. Let's begin today with everyone participating where they can be helpful. Call your parish and enlist in the effort to grow parishes. Ask them where they need help. Call your Catholic friends and get a group together to discover how you want to contribute. Then, meet with your priest.

> *Lord, have mercy upon us and upon the whole Church. Guide us by your Holy Spirit to heal and revitalize the Church. Amen.*

> *One hundred percent of the proceeds of this book will be given to build ministries in the Catholic Parish where the books are sold.*

Marijka is available to visit parishes with the results of the research findings and to help grow and heal your parish.

Feel free to write

marijkalampard@gmail.com

APPENDIX

T he following is an example of a parish handbook from St. John Vianney Parish, Orchard Park, NY. It is reproduced here with permission.

WHO DO YOU CALL FOR _?

• Requests for Baptisms, Weddings, Memorials and Funerals	Contact Name Phone # Email address
• Anointing of the Sick & Dying	
• Recommendation Letters	
• Mass Intentions	
• Registering for the Parish	
• Bulletin Information	

• Scheduling a room • Bulletin notice • Financial	Contact Name Phone # Email address
• Becoming a Catholic / RCIA	Contact Name Phone # Email address
• Early Childhood Education (PK) • Elementary School (K-8)	Contact Name Phone # Email address
• Sacraments for Children	Contact Name Phone # Email address

Website Information

www.saintjohnvianney.com

ALCOHOLIC ANONYMOUS (MONDAY GROUP)

Service to Parish: Alcoholic Anonymous (AA) is a recovery group for alcoholics who are often spiritually bankrupt. When recovered they are restored to a childhood faith. Although not a formal ministry, St. John Vianney Parish is happy to host this organization.

Special Events: Spiritual weekend at the Christ the King Seminary

Meeting Time and Location: Mondays at 3:30 PM in the SJV Church Gathering Room and Chapel.

Contact Name / Phone # / Email address

ALCOHOLIC ANONYMOUS (WEDNESDAY GROUP)

Service to Parish: Alcoholic Anonymous (AA) is a fellowship of men and women who share their experience, strength and hope with each other to help solve their common problems and help others to recover from alcoholism. Although not a formal ministry, St. John Vianney Parish is happy to host this organization.

Special Events: None

Meeting Time and Location: Wednesdays at 4:00 PM in the SJV Church Gathering Room

ALTAR SERVERS

Service to Parish: To serve at weekly parish masses and weddings.

Special Events: None

Meeting Time and Location: Weekly parish masses are assigned and include a yearly training. Altar servers will be scheduled 2-3 times per calendar quarter or up to 12 times per year. Holy Week, Christmas and Easter schedules are on a volunteer basis.

Contact Name / Phone # / Email address

BAPTISM PREPARATION

Service to Parish: "Baptism is the door to the Spiritual life. To be Christian is to share in the relationship that Jesus has with the Father and to help bring others to share in that Life."

For parents seeking Baptism for their child: A prerequisite for your child's baptism, St. John Vianney hosts a Pre-Baptism Session as our way of helping you enter this special moment as fully excited and informed about the Sacrament as possible. We see this session as an opportunity to make the "Baptism Experience" a rich family faith experience. Sessions last approximately an hour and a half.

Special Events: None

Meeting Time and Location: Per appointment with Rectory

For Parishioners interested in Baptismal Ministry Leadership: Pre- Baptism preparation and formation, for couples seeking baptism for their child, is an important parish ministry! We ask our parishioners to prayerfully consider whether God might be calling you to give of your time and talent as Pre-Baptism Session Facilitators/ Coordinators. Training is available.

Contact Name / Phone # / Email address

BOY SCOUTS TROOP 1776 (AGES 11-18); CUB SCOUTS (AGES 6-10)

Service to Parish: To provide the Easter Vigil fire and planting flowers for the SJV veteran memorial. Although not a formal ministry, St. John Vianney Parish is happy to host this organization.

Special Events: Pancake Breakfast in the Fall; Spaghetti Dinner and Food Drive in the Spring.

Meeting Time and Location: Wednesday evenings from 7:00- 8:45 PM in the SJV School cafeteria

Contact Name / Phone # / Email address

CHILDREN'S LITURGY

Service to Parish: To provide children of the Parish an opportunity to hear the Sunday readings and Gospel of the Mass from the Lectionary for Masses with Children. Two groups of children (ages 4-5; ages 6+) are dismissed from Liturgy of the Word during the 10 AM Sunday Mass to go to the Chapel and Gathering Room with teachers and aides. They experience the parts of the Mass on their level of understanding, returning to the congregation after the Prayer of the Faithful. Some children take part in the Offertory procession.

Special Events: None

Meeting Time and Location: First and third Sundays of the month at the 10 AM Mass.

Contact Name / Phone # / Email address

Church Cleaning

Service to Parish: To provide weekly cleaning of Church

Special Events: None

Meeting Time and Location: Weekly on Thursday mornings from 6:00 to 8:00 AM

Contact Name / Phone # / Email address

Church Ushers

Service to Parish: To serve the worshiping community by greeting and seating people, taking up the offertory collection, distributing the bulletins and assisting with the needs of the assembly.

Special Events: Confirmations

Meeting Time and Location: Ushers are assigned to designated Masses on a weekly basis

Contact Name / Phone # / Email address

Collection Counters

Service to Parish: Assist in the counting of weekly and special collections. Members are selected by the Pastor. Volunteers are assigned to one of six teams and will be asked to serve one time every other month for 2 to 4 hours.

Special Events: None

Meeting Time and Location: Church Rectory.

Contact Name / Phone # / Email address

COMMUNION TO THE SICK

Service to Parish: To provide communion every Sunday after 10 AM Mass to homebound parishioners and area independent senior facilities.

Special Events: None

Meeting Time and Location: Assignments are provided monthly by mail and posted in Church sacristy each week. Members should expect to serve one Sunday every month.

Contact Name / Phone # / Email address

DAUGHTERS AND SONS OF RUTH

Service to Parish: To provide a luncheon for parish families and friends following funerals.

Special Events: None

Meeting Time and Location: There are no formal meetings. Volunteers listings will be called and volunteers will be asked to provide a prepared dish or other food items for the bereavement meal. Bereavement meal set up and cleanup will require 3-4 hours of volunteer time.

Contact Name / Phone # / Email address

ENGAGED COUPLE MARRIAGE PREPARATION PROGRAM

Service to Parish: To prepare engaged couples for marriage. Special Events: None

Meeting Time and Location: Meetings are scheduled in the evenings with the engaged couples. Commitment time will vary.

Contact Name / Phone # / Email address

EUCHARISTIC MINISTERS

Service to Parish: To serve at masses with distribution of the body and blood of Christ.

Special Events: None

Meeting Time and Location: There are no formal meetings. Interested parishioners are welcome to become Eucharistic Ministers and are required to attend a one day training session. Eucharistic minister schedules are made available quarterly and distributed via email (if provided) or mailed. Volunteers will be expected to serve 12 times per year.

Contact Name / Phone # / Email address

FAITH SHARING

Service to Parish: A new ministry which provides faith sharing opportunities among parishioners.

Special Events: None

Meeting Time and Location: Every 6 weeks for 1 ½ hours. Location will vary according to who is hosting.

Contact Name / Phone # / Email address

FAMILY FAITH FORMATION

Service to Parish: To provide religious education for children and youth in grades 1 through grade 10 including preparation for First Reconciliation, First Communion and Confirmation. New catechists to provide instruction and formation opportunities are always needed and welcome.

Special Events: First Reconciliation, First Eucharist, Confirmation and retreats for all three sacraments.

Meeting Time and Location: Monday/Tuesday/Thursday evenings and Saturday mornings at SJV School during the school year. Volunteers will be asked to commit to 1 ½ hours per class.

Contact Name / Phone # / Email address

FINANCE COMMITTEE

Service to Parish: To provide Parish financial oversight and planning. The committee is comprised of seven members who provide service 3 hours per month.

Special Events: None

Meeting Time and Location: Monthly in the SJV Church Rectory

Contact Name / Phone # / Email address

GARDENING GROUP

Service to Parish: Our energetic group prepares, plants flowers and maintains the Church, Rectory and School flower gardens and planters from May through October. Once the spring planting is complete the group meets every two weeks for 2 hours to provide garden maintenance.

Special Events: Plant Booth at SJV Lawn Fete in July.

Meeting Time and Location: Every other Tuesday from May until October.

Contact Name / Phone # / Email address

HOLY NAME SOCIETY

Service to Parish: To provide financial assistance to parish and school based on profits made from various functions and raffl es. Special Events: Yearly Mass, Football Championship Sunday, Bowling Party, Cookout, Golf Outing, Baseball Excursion, Nite at Buffalo Raceway,

Buffalo Bills season ticket raffle, 200 Club Raffle for school tuition assistance.

Meeting Time and Location: Monthly meeting first Tuesday of each month in Joan Wedgwood Center. Meetings take place year round. Members should expect to participate approximately 1 hour per month.

Contact Name / Phone # / Email address

HOME SCHOOL ASSOCIATION

Service to Parish: To provide funds to the parish to offset tuition cost.

Special Events: Various fundraisers to provide subsidy to the parish which includes the Meat Raffle and Cash Giveaway Party.

Meeting Time and Location: Monthly in the Joan Wedgwood Center. The organization president provides 20 hours of service per month. The vice-president and secretary provide 3 hours of service per month. All positions are 2 year terms.

Contact Name / Phone # / Email address

HOSPITALITY/GREETERS

Service to Parish: To welcome parishioners and guests before and after weekend Masses. Greeters are available to answer questions and hand out information when necessary.

Special Events: None

Meeting Time and Location: There are no formal meetings but individual parishioners and parish families are welcome to become greeters. Volunteers should expect to spend 45 minutes to attend and greet parishioners before and after their assigned mass.

Contact Name / Phone # / Email address

Knights of St. John

Service to the Parish: To participate in special liturgies and provide help in Parish projects.

Special Events: Annual Chicken BBQ on first Sunday in May. Meeting Time and Location: Mass and meeting in Joan Wedgwood Center on first Wednesday of the month. Members can expect to participate approximately 1 hour each month.

Contact Name / Phone # / Email address

Lawn Fete

Service to Parish: This is a major Parish fundraiser with profits used to offset Parish expenses. The Lawn Fete includes music, food, games and a 5K run. Many volunteers are needed for this event.

Special Events: The event includes an annual 5K run, beer tent, gambling tent, dinners, children's tent, basket raffle, cruise night and bands.

Meeting Time and Location: The Lawn Fete is in July on the Parish grounds.

Contact Name / Phone # / Email address

LECTORS

Service to Parish: To proclaim God's Word in the Scripture readings to the parish community at Sunday, Holiday and Holy Day of Obligation masses. In addition to proclaiming the first and second readings, lectors welcome the parish community at the beginning of Mass and read the Parish announcements at the end of Mass.

Special Events: None

Meeting Time and Location: There are no formal meetings. Interested parishioners are welcome to become Lectors and are required to attend a one day training session. Lector schedules are made available quarterly and distributed via email (if provided) or mailed. Lectors should expect to serve 8 times per year.

Contact Name / Phone # / Email address

MUSIC MINISTRY/CHOIR

Service to Parish: We now have three choirs plus our wonderful cantors and musicians to provide ministry through music at all our masses. Our main choir mass is generally at the 10 AM mass on Sunday. This would be either our Adult or Children's Choir who sings once per month. Our newly formed Teen Choir practice 11 am on Sundays and sing at the 10 am mass on the last Sunday of the month. Our other masses are cantor/musician led.

Special Events: Lessons and Carols

Meeting Time and Location: The choir practices every Wednesday from 6:30-8:30 PM and Sunday mornings at 9:15 AM.

Contact Name / Phone # / Email address

PARISH TRUSTEES

Service to Parish: To provide fiduciary preservation and care guidance of Parish property in addition to assisting the Pastor with Parish issues. Trustees are appointed by the Pastor.

Special Events: None

Meeting Time and Location: As scheduled by the Pastor. Meetings generally take place in the SJV Rectory.

Contact Name / Phone # / Email address

PRAYER SHAWL GROUP

Service to Parish: Making prayer shawls, lap robes and baby blankets for those in need.

Special Events: Prayer Shawl Sunday occurs annually which allows parishioners to take a shawl for individuals in need of comfort, prayer and support.

Meeting Time and Location: Meetings are held on the third Thursday of the month in the Church Gathering Room from 8:30 AM to 10:30 AM.

Contact Name / Phone # / Email address

PRO-LIFE/RESPECT LIFE

Service to Parish: To promote the spiritual and physical welfare of all from conception to the end of life.

Special Events: Diaper Drive for Gianna Molla Pregnancy Outreach Center, Awareness-Baby Crisis, National Night of Prayer

Meeting Time and Location: Attend events sponsored by other parishes. There are no definite meeting dates or times.

Contact Name / Phone # / Email address

RCIA

Service to Parish: The members of the RCIA team share their faith through Scripture with Catechumens (people who want to become Catholics) and Candidates (people who have received the sacrament of Baptism but need the sacraments of Eucharist and Confirmation).

Special Events: None

Meeting Time and Location: Weekly meetings are held in the Church Gathering Room. Volunteers and team members will be asked to serve 2 hours per week from September to May.

Contact Name / Phone # / Email address

Saint John Vianney School

Service to Parish: To provide a Roman Catholic education rooted in spiritual development, service and academic rigors in grades Pre-Kindergarten (ages 3 and 4) to Grade 8.

Special Events: Meat Raffle, Cash Giveaway, grade level service, Halloween Party, annual Gala, Thanksgiving Feast.

Meeting Time and Location: September to June, Monday through Friday 8:30 AM to 2:50 PM. **Summer hours:** Monday to Thursday, 9 AM to 2 PM. Contact Name / Phone # / Email address

Senior Citizens

Service to Parish: Members volunteer to support various Parish activities.

Special Events: Luncheons, pizza parties, ice cream socials, picnics and programs with speakers.

Meeting Time and Location: Meetings are the second and fourth Tuesdays of the month from 12:30 PM to 3:30 PM in the Joan Wedgwood Center.

Contact Name / Phone # / Email address

SILENT ANGELS

Service to Parish: Helping to direct those in need to the appropriate agencies, assisting those in need in the Parish and supporting several area food pantries.

Meeting Time and Location: Presently there are no specific meeting dates. We are looking for new members so we can begin meeting on a regular basis.

The annual SJV Thanksgiving Day Mass collection is donated to the cause of aiding the needy of our Parish. The food collection at this Mass is donated to helping the needy of our Parish during the holiday season.

Contact Name / Phone # / Email address

SODALITY OF OUR LADY

Service to Parish: Our Sodality is primarily a religious and parochial organization. Our loyalty is to the Blessed Virgin Mary and to our Parish. The object and purpose of this organization is to lend itself to spiritual devotions and any enterprise. Our enterprises are connected with necessary funds for the Church and are involved with the liturgy, parish and any other fund raising organizations. Members participate in meetings for 2 hours per month with the option to choose from 10-12 ministries within the organization for additional volunteer opportunities.

Special Events: Our goal is to provide two (2) major fund raisers each year (Fall & Spring) to help our Parish

Community in raising funds to be used where needs are most great.

Meeting Time and Location: Meetings are held on the 3rd Tuesday of the month from September to June in the Joan Wedgwood Center.

Contact Name / Phone # / Email address

VITALITY COMMITTEE

Service to the Parish: To create a parish mission and vision and to assist the parish in continued development and formation of a church culture of intentional discipleship in response to the challenge of Jesus to "go and make disciples". There is no formal process for soliciting new members.

Special Events: Enhancing our Parish faith life through special hospitality, outreach and spiritual events.

Meeting Time and Location: Dates and times vary but generally meet monthly in the SJV Gathering Room for 2-3 hours. Additional subcommittee meetings are held as needed.

Contact Name / Phone # / Email address

WOMEN'S DISCUSSION GROUP

Service to Parish: To provide a forum for discussion among parish women of all ages. A prepared agenda guides the meeting discussion.

Special Events: Dinner in June

Meeting Time and Location: Meeting are held the second Thursday of the month from October through May in the SJV Church Gathering Room. Meetings are 2 ½ hours. Times vary.

Contact Name / Phone # / Email address

ADDITIONAL FAITH SHARING OPPORTUNITIES:

Daily: Recitation of the Rosary followed by Divine Mercy Chaplet after 8 AM Mass Monday, Tuesday, Thursday and Friday

Weekly: Mass and ministry to developmentally disabled adults (18 years+). Contact Fr. Bob through Rectory office (674-9133) for information

Bimonthly: Faith Workshop. Thursdays from 10:30 AM-12:00 PM

Bimonthly: Children's Liturgy. 1st and 3rd Sunday 10 AM Mass throughout the school year

Bimonthly: Eucharistic Adoration (check bulletin)

March: St. Joseph's Table

Celtic Mass

Lent: Stations of the Cross every Friday evening

April to October: Symbolon

May: Veteran's Memorial Mass.10 AM Mass last Sunday of May

November: Mass of Remembrance.7 PM

December: Lessons and Carols

ORGANIZATION	CONTACT	PHONE	EMAIL ADDRESS
Alcoholics Anonymous	Name	XXX-XXXX	
Altar Servers			
Baptism Preparation			
Boy Scouts Troop 1776			
Children's Liturgy			
Church Cleaning			
Church Ushers			
Collection Counters			
Communion to Sick			
Daughters and Sons of Ruth			
Engaged Couple Marriage Preparation Program			
Eucharistic Minister			
Faith Sharing Group			
Family Faith Formation Program			
Finance Committee			
Gardening Group			
Holy Name Society			
Home School Association			

ORGANIZATION	CONTACT	PHONE	EMAIL ADDRESS
Hospitality/Greeters			
Knights of St. John			
Lawn Fete			
Lectors			
Music Ministry/Choir			
Parish Trustees			
Prayer Shawl			
Pro-Life/Respect Life Committee			
RCIA			
Senior Citizens			
Silent Angels			
SJV School Principal			
Sodality of Our Lady			
Vitality Committee			
Women's Discussion Group			

St. Matthew's Church, Charlotte, North Carolina, offers many ministries. I have included this list here as an example of the possibilities that exist for parishes:

A Child's Place

Adult Faith Formation

Altar Guild

Altar Servers

Angel Tree

Arts & Environment

AV Committee

Bereavement Ministry

Blood Give-In

Bowling (Couples)

Bowling (Ladies)

Boy Scouts

Bridge

Cenacles of Divine Mercy

Centering Prayer

Charismatic Prayer Group

Children's Choir

Children's' Liturgy of the Word

Christ Renews His Parish

Christian Responders

Christian Coffeehouse

Christians in Career Transition

Columbiettes

CROP Walk

Cub Scouts

Cursillo

Disaster Shelter Team

Donated Goods

Elizabeth Ministry

Engagement Outreach

Eucharistic Adoration

Extraordinary Ministers of Holy Communion

Family Assist

Family Connection Ministry

Family Life Ministry

Finance Council

First Fridays

Food Pantry

Friendship Trays

Funeral Receptions

Girl Scouts

Habitat for Humanity

Homeless Relief Ministry

Homemakers of Mercy

Hospice Meals

Knights of Columbus

Knit and Crochet

Lectio Divina

Legion of Mary

Library Committee

Living Your Strengths

Lunch to Go

Mass Greeters

Mel's Diner

Men's Shelter– Tryon Campus

Men's Shelter– Statesville Campus

Ministers of the Word

Ministers to Assisted Living/Nursing Homes

Ministers to Hospitals

Ministers to Homebound

Ministry to the Deaf

Moms Group

Muffin Ministry

Music Ministry

New Ventures

Newcomers' Group-Moving On After Moving In

Our Daily Bread

Our Lady's Rosary Makers Guild

Pastoral Council

Peace and Justice Committee

Pinochle Club

Prayer Line

RCIA

RCIA for Teens

REACH

Refugee Resettlement

Respect Life

Sacristans

Sandwich Programs

Seams of Faith

Seeking Purpose

Softball

SPRED

St. Matthew Mom's Group

STARs (Seniors)

Stewardship Committee

Strengths Coaching

Strengths Quest

Teams of Our Lady

Ushers

Vocations Awareness

Welcome Desk

Welcome Home for Returning Catholics

WelcomeMatt

Welcoming Committee

World Hunger Drive

Youth Sports (Basketball)

Young Adult Ministries

Prayer is central at St. Matthew's Church and here are some of their programs for Spiritual Life & Prayer

- Cenacles of The Divine Mercy

- Centering Prayer

- Charismatic Prayer Group

- Eucharistic Adoration

- Lectio Divina

- Legion of Mary

- Prayer Line

- Seeking Purpose

- St. Matthew Moms Group

- Strengths Coaching

- Teams of Our Lady

- Vocations Awareness Ministry

ACKNOWLEDGMENTS

Thanks to those who contributed in the book as referenced.

The information and thoughts in this book are for consideration and are not necessarily the reflections of those acknowledged as follows.

Dr. John Hurley

Fr. Binoy Davis

Fr. David Tourville

Carolyn Klicka

Dr. Maureen Hurley

Anita Price

Dave and Sharon Walsh

Fr. Marc Roselli

Fr. Dominik Jezierski

Deacon Paul Snyder

Fr. Jan Trela

Charlie Specht

John Lampard

Marijka Christina Lampard

Fr. Dennis Mende

Fr. Larry Richards

Janet Vant

Fr. Tim Koester

Fr. Mark Noonan

Fr. Patrick Elis

Shiobhan O'Connor

Fr. Robert Zilliox

Mary Beth (Baker) Giltner

Don Garbison

Fr. Darrell Duffy

Kathleen McGough Johnson

Jos, Femy and Ellen Van Domburg

REFERENCES AND RESOURCES

Barron, Robert. Letter to a Suffering Church. Park Ridge IL: Word on Fire Catholic Ministries, 2019.

Bullivant, Stephen. Catholicism in the Time of Coronavirus. Word on Fire Podcast, 2020.

Hahn, Scott. A Father Who Keeps His Promises. Cincinnati, OH. Servant Books, 1998.

Hahn, Scott. The Lamb's Supper. New York, NY. Doubleday, 1999.

Landry, Scot. Transforming Parish Communications. Huntington, Indiana, Our Sunday Visitor, Inc. 2014.

Lindsey, David. The Woman and the Dragon. Gretna, Louisiana. Pelican Publishing, 2000.

Michalenko, Seraphim. The Divine Mercy Message and Devotion. Stockbridge, MA. Marian Press, 2004.

Schneider, Athanasius. Christus Vincit. Brooklyn, NY, Angelico Press, 2019.

Simon, William E. Great Catholic Parishes. Notre Dame, IN, Ave Maria Press, 2016.

Wesley, Christopher. Rebuilding Youth Ministry. Notre Dame, IN, Ave Maria Press,2015.

White, Michael and Tom Corcoran. Rebuilding Your Message. Notre Dame, IN, Ave Maria Press, 2015.

White, Michael and Tom Corcoran. Church Money. Notre Dame, IN, Ave Maria Press, 2019.

White, Michael and Tom Corcoran. Rebuilt. Notre Dame, IN, Ave Maria Press, 2013.

White, Michael and Tom Corcoran. Tools for Rebuilding. Notre Dame, IN, Ave Maria Press, 2013.

So Pastor, What's Your Point? On Kindle at Amazonbooks. com, 2013.

Movement to Restore Trust (MRT) https://www.canisius. edu/

Catechism of the Catholic Church. New York, NY, Libreria Editrice Vaticana 1994.

ABOUT THE
AUTHOR

Marijka E. Lampard

B orn of immigrant parents from the Netherlands who arrived in Halifax, Nova Scotia in 1950, I grew up in Markham, Ontario. I went to Catholic schools all my life. St Joseph's Morrow Park high school was the all-girls school in the outskirts of Toronto, run by the Sisters of St. Joseph. My four younger brothers went to the boys' Jesuit high school called St. John Brebeuf around the corner. I learned how to get along with guys and they played a strong part in my formative years. I loved to learn and was an avid reader.

Growing up in the country, Church was a weekend highlight, although we often had Mass at school. The Mass for me was transcendence spiritually to a heavenly realm, on waves of powerful prayers of the Mass. Although in Latin, I followed the right side of the missal because my Latin was not advanced enough. After high school, I went to the University of Waterloo, Ontario and to the University of Calgary, Alberta and took environmental and planning graduate programs. I started the youth group at my small church in Markham. That was the extent of my contribution to the Church in my formative years.

I married a family practitioner physician happily at first. After marrying in the Catholic Church, we did not attend the Catholic Church because it wasn't his thing. Throughout the 17 years of marriage, we church shopped, ending up mostly in the Baptist church or evangelica churches, and I would hear from the congregation encour aging me, "Now you can have a personal relationship witl Jesus Christ, you can rest assured that you can have sal vation forever if you say the sinners prayer and give your heart to Jesus." They kept reminding me that Catholics are not saved. For years I tolerated this notion while my mind struggled with the fact that I had received all the Sacraments and was keen on my relationship with God. "Have you ever given your heart to Jesus," they kept asking and I'm thinking Catholics give their lives to Christ, not just their hearts. Sometimes, they do not know how to show it. It was disconcerting and confusing while I spent over 10 years in the Protestant church.

There were benefits to my Protestant journey. I learned to pray out loud and pray from the heart. Scripture was dwelled on and made applicable. Even the little children in nursery were taught to memorize scripture verses.

There were drawbacks too. I learned it was not a good idea to pray to Mary or to the saints. And over the years I found my heart hardening towards Mary. I felt like a hypocrite in the pew partaking of the crackers and grape juice for communion service. I did love my fellow Christians in the pews but puzzled at their lack of reverence for God. This was evident by their dress code on stage and their secular dance moves during worship music. They took great pride in praying to God for one another telling God exactly what they wanted Him to do and how. "Name it and claim it" they would pray. I could not tell God what to do.

My husband joined the Church of Scientology and within two years our marriage was terminated. Our families and friends could not free him from the stranglehold of Scientology. Despite attending courses in San Francisco at the Church of Scientology, after months of indoctrination, I escaped and went home. I ran back to the Catholic Church. It was my comfort, my solace, my rescue.

Over the years, I realized I had returned to a Catholic Church with problems, but I knew I could not leave again. I fell in love with the Sacraments all over again, and through spiritual guidance and a very long confession, I searched and found good people, a beautiful Mass, nourishing Homilies, and an opportunity to lead Bible study, which fed my soul as well.

Fast forward 30 years, I had used my planning skills to work for Kaleida Health as a hospital planner. I began my own hospital consulting company that prospered. I sold the company to my two sons and then I enjoyed retirement for a couple of years.

Meanwhile, I had done Eucharistic ministry which was very fulfilling, visiting the sick and homebound and sharing Christ with them. I had participated in many Bible studies; led many Bible studies and that was a great fellowship time, and growing in Christ. I loved to do funeral breakfasts. For me it was an honor to pray at the funeral Mass for the soul of the deceased and to offer solace to others while serving breakfast. I served on Parish Council for two terms. My three children were with me in Church and they received all of the Sacraments and continued to be strong in their faith.

Compelled to respond to the grave turmoil caused by the sex scandals in the diocese of Buffalo, the pews emptying in my own parish, collections falling, my friend Kathleen McGough Johnson and I responded to a letter in the Buffalo news written by President John Hurley of Canisius College. He announced that it was the laity that would restore the Church. We became the first of thirty people to form MRT (Movement to Restore Trust) in the Buffalo diocese. This group is now comprised of 150 very intelligent and skilled, devote Catholics. Through listening sessions at parishes and parish research we did on our own, this book hopefully will help to restore trust in the catholic parish.

I do not have all of the answers, and this book cannot have all of the answers. It does, however, pose great topics for discussion, and a call for wisdom and discernment leading to action.

It is a call to all baptized in the Catholic faith to respond as best they can to fix the problems, and not to lose heart. It is also by Cannon law your right to do so. This book will help to show you how. Come help save the Church, for Jesus saved you first.

Feel free to send me a note:
marijkalampard@gmail.com

God Bless You